3Bg6

GEORGE MEREDITH

GEORGE MEREDITH

Selected Poems

Edited with an introduction and notes by Keith Hanley

Fyfield Books

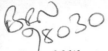

ACKNOWLEDGEMENTS

I would like to thank my friends Roger Holdsworth, Bernard and Heather O'Donoghue, Sara Pearl and Nina Sergelius for urging, and in different ways improving, this selection. I am particularly grateful to John Stachniewski who read through the manuscript and made some shrewd suggestions and corrections. Campbell Thomson & McLaughlin Ltd. have kindly permitted me to print material from MSS in their ownership.

First published in 1983
Published in new format 1988 by
Carcanet Press Limited
208–212 Corn Exchange Buildings
Manchester M4 3BQ
and 198 Sixth Avenue
New York, NY 10013

British Library Cataloguing in Publication Data
Meredith, George
Selected Poems. — (Fyfield)
I. Title   II. Hanley, Keith   III. Series
821'.8   PR

ISBN: 0-85635-416-3

The publisher acknowledges financial assistance
from the Arts Council of Great Britain.

Printed in England by SRP Ltd, Exeter.

In Memory of Kitty Baxendale

CONTENTS

I LIFE

George Meredith was born in Portsmouth in 1828. He liked to emphasize his Celtic ancestry—the Welsh and possibly Irish blood—and to deflect attention from his ungenteel social origins, as the son and grandson of tailors engaged in trade. As a result of family legacies he was educated for a year and a half by the Moravian Brotherhood at Neuwied in Germany who introduced him to ideals of self-respect and human co-operation less constricting than those of the Victorian middle classes. Nevertheless, his social outlook became a curious blending of democratic reformism and high breeding—so oddly compatible for the nineteenth-century liberal. Chesterton captures him nicely, with one foot in the woods and the other in the drawing-room, 'a sort of daintily dressed Walt Whitman' (1).

He read for the bar, but in search of a regular income he turned to journalism and then to reading for the publishers, Chapman and Hall. These avocations kept him in the literary swim: early on, he received the personal counsels of the older Carlyle, and later he extended his own to the young Hardy who forty years after elegized him memorably: 'His note was trenchant, turning kind.' (2)

The financial insecurity caused by his insistence on pursuing a literary career was one factor in the undermining of his first marriage to Mary Ellen Nicolls, daughter of the gourmet satirist Thomas Love Peacock. She was over six years older than the twenty-one year old Meredith, a widow with a daughter from the previous marriage. But she was a highly cultivated product of her father's milieu, a published poet, and was regarded in her circle as a very attractive wit. They had only one surviving child, Arthur Gryffydh, before their highly-strung and economically hampered relationship deteriorated into Mary's infidelity and elopement to Capri with a minor Pre-Raphaelite painter, Henry Wallis. Mary returned to England, begged to see the child, but was refused. When she became fatally ill Meredith allowed her to see the child but, implacable to the end, never visited her, nor attended the funeral. It was the crucial relationship of his life, and his feelings were channelled immediately into literary reactions:

The Ordeal of Richard Feverel was written after her desertion in 1858, and *Modern Love* after her death in 1861.

He married again, this time happily. As his second wife he chose Marie Vulliamy, the placid Anglo-French daughter of a retired French industrialist. In 1864 they set up home at Flint Cottage, Box Hill, Surrey, where Meredith wrote the series of novels which confirmed his reputation, including *The Egoist* (1879) and *Diana of the Crossways* (1885). In the countryside around he organized the walking tours which became a sort of athletic cult, and gradually established himself as a literary guru, visited by pilgrim artists and statesmen. As his fame grew, the doctrines, with which he was late-Victorian enough to infuse his works, began to date. In his last years Shaw found him 'a relic of the Cosmopolitan Republican Gentleman of the previous generation.' (3)

His death in 1909—Swinburne had died earlier that year—marked the official end of a period of modern transition to which he had made his significant contribution long before in the previous century. Now Yeats proclaimed himself 'King of the Cats' (4).

II THOUGHT

Meredith's optimistic naturalism is never complacent, however doctrinaire and sometimes patly expressed it becomes in the 1880s. It is the result of a strenuous imaginative effort to confront a modern sense of tragedy. He shares the realization that horrifies Tennyson in *In Memoriam*, of a nature 'careless of the single life' (1); he acknowledges man's evolutionary descent and the Darwinian struggles for survival. His name for these natural conditions is 'Earth', and he tries to invent ways of 'reading' her that can give meaning to the experience of human life, encouraged to do so by a temperamental intuition that the conditions are finally good, that living is worthwhile.

On the assumption, then, that Earth is good he tries to discover her laws, to see as positives, to which man must learn to bow, the seemingly incontrovertible findings of science. He attempts to humanize them in the context in which they increasingly threatened to dehumanize his society: his first book of poems came out in the year of the Great Exhibition, and he died in the year Wells published *Tono-Bungay*. In all this he is fulfilling the Wordsworthian poetic mission of discerning 'the impassioned expression which is in the countenance of all Science', and of 'carrying everywhere with him relationship and love.' (2) Admittedly the expression can sometimes become stoically fixed, to drive home central, hard, paradoxical tenets such as the need to derive a thrill of joy from the apparent cruelties of evolutionary contention—urging 'a creature matched with strife,/To meet it as a bride'.(3) But the earnestness of the nature poetry is generally a constructive attempt to identify the components of a resilient modern personality, whereas the social comedy of his novels mostly mocks the characters' inability, through sentimentality or self-importance, to attain it. Directly and by implication, his works promote the desire for the kind of society described in his lecture-essay, 'The Idea of Comedy and the Uses of the Comic Spirit', in which both men and women are intelligent enough to laugh at their human short-comings, and to work critically to improve them.

E. M. Forster, who owed more to the Meredithian invention of 'the home counties posing as the universe' than he seems to realize, claims that 'What is really tragic and enduring in the scenery of England was hidden from him, and so is what is really tragic in life.' (4) There are, however, poems in which Meredith's personal sense of loss proves insuppressible, as in his elegy on his second wife, 'Change in Recurrence', where the obliviousness of nature, as in Wordsworth's Lucy poems, is poised with his subjective grief. 'The Thrush in February' is similarly an heroic attempt to dramatize his theory of acceptance in the face of his wife's imminent painful death. There is, in fact, in all his best nature poetry an impression of imaginative investigation and effort that never totally loses contact with the beleaguered humanism of *Modern Love*, where awareness of a natural hostility can be placated only by the most resourceful strategies.

His solution was to fabricate a vision of an impersonal humane will that transcends individuality, propelled in his attempt by responsibility for a communal sense of tragedy:

> I did believe I stood alone,
> Till that great company of Grief
> Taught me to know this craving heart
> For not my own. (5)

Even the rigorous dogmatism, influenced by the Carlylean doctrine of Work, is conceived as an active contribution to the spread of rationality, offered in the conviction that 'Philosophy is Life's one match for Fate.' (6) In this way he redefines Wordsworth's ethical formulation of an impersonal duty, his 'second Will more wise' (7), in terms specifically of Comtean altruism:

> You a larger self will find:
> Sweetest fellowship ensues
> With the creatures of your kind. (8)

The rather heady conclusion is a sort of completely socialized survival of the self: 'life begets with fair increase / Beyond the flesh, if life be true.' (9)

The will to rational optimism involves a departure from Darwinian principles and reliance on another, pre-Darwinian tradition of evolution associated with Goethe's theory of perpetual vital change. Goethe had suggested that there is in the natural process of change an inherent principle of sanity and order towards which nature evolves and in which man is actively trained, but not individually determined. With the help of reason, man may choose to conform or else to be destroyed: 'Her Lord, if to her rigid laws he bows; / Her dust, if with his conscience he plays knave'. (10)

The crucial opposition is to Darwin's belief that self-preservation is the basis of the evolutionary urge. For Meredith it is precisely what he understands as the self that disables the vision of a whole society into which he urges individuals should evolve. His model for the evolution of human personality is the triad elaborated in 'The Woods of Westermain': 'Blood and brain and spirit, three . . . Join for true felicity.' (11) The components correspond to selfish sensationalism, rational intelligence and social altruism; and the chief threat comes from the over-assertion of the selfish, 'id'-like blood that must constantly be developed into the higher capacities. Reason and altruism, Meredith often suggests, are potential in physical sensations: 'Pleasures that through blood run sane, / Quickening spirit from the brain.' (12) His poems often amount to descriptions of the transition contained in the propositions that 'Life thoroughly lived is a fact in the brain' (13), and that the jubilant song of the ascending lark communicates its inspiration to the 'warriors' of modern society 'In the brain's reflex of yon bird'. (14) Many of his poems show him losing self-consciousness in the struggling energies of natural process, so that the energies become an impersonal life-giving force that evokes, with its idealistic-materialist ambivalence, both the German idealists and Bergson:

> Flame, stream, we are, in mid career
> From torrent source, delirious dream,
> To heaven-reflecting currents clear. (15)

In the integration of 'the larger self', reason, or human intelligence, mediates between the Life of selfish sensation and Death into altruism. As well as the relegation of the sensing self, a positive exploration of the possible human meanings of Earth is essential to the programme. The point, in the course of the exercise, becomes no longer to what extent these meanings proceed from Earth, but whether the perceiving mind can create from the common conditions of natural experience symbols of its own power to transcend selfish individualism, and still preserve a conviction of human value. The mind is willing contentedly to surrender its self-consciousness and 'attain the glee / Of things without a destiny!' (16) when it can find recognizably good, that is of shared human value, what it will no longer be able to observe in detachment. The point of a consolation such as: 'Into the breast that gives the rose, / Shall I with shuddering fall?' (17) is not just that Earth is good to produce what he enjoys with his senses in the living moment, but that the flower is an agreed symbol of the human perception of a kind of natural perfection: 'Change is on the wing to bud / Rose in brain from rose in blood.' (18)

Certain moods of nature seem to promise a sense of integration that requires no probing, as in the contented agnosticism (19) of 'Woodland Peace':

> what is dumb,
> We question not, nor ask
> The silent to give sound. (20)

In other poems there is a bristling awareness that the scene is fraught with seemingly immanent messages, as in the delicately generalized intuition of human import which pervades 'Night of Frost in May':

What serious breath the woodland drew;
The low throb of expectancy;
How the white mother-muteness pressed
On leaf and meadow-herb .... (21)

At such times, when he is 'calmly bent / To read the lines dear Earth designs' (22), the implication becomes explicit that it is his representative human perception that establishes their value:

They have no song, the sedges dry,
    And still they sing.
It is within my heart they sing,
    As I pass by. (23)

His poetry is itself designed to amplify and frame these human values, to sustain the possibility of perception of optimistic naturalism, according to 'The cry of the conscience of Life' he raises in his seventies: *'Keep the young generation in hail, / And bequeath them no tumbled house!'* (24)

III STYLE

Meredith's is demanding verse, and, as he himself predicted of *Modern Love*, it can only be properly understood 'by the few who would read it many times.' (1) There are several styles and a great variety of forms, but they are all characterized by a striking experimentalism. As Lionel Stevenson remarks, *Poems and Lyrics*, 1883, was, after a virtual poetic silence of over twenty years, 'the most powerful and original volume of poetry that had appeared in a decade.' (2) Thereafter the experimental nature of his style hardened, and by the 1890s had lost its feel of lively exploration—a tendency Trevelyan attributes 'in part to the want of public attention and appreciative criticism during the years when his style was being formed.' (3)

There is a common effect of obscurity throughout the different kinds of verse, whether they are concerned with nature description, the aphoristic transmission of his philosophy, or telling a story, as in the later ballads. Descriptive poems like 'Ode to the Spirit of Earth in Autumn' fuse streams of loosely connected metaphors in the general evocation of a natural scene. Philosophical poems like 'The

Woods of Westermain' comprise strings of gnomic sayings connected by a running allegory of the woods standing for life. The later ballads, like 'King Harald's Trance', are halting narratives with motives and key events often entirely omitted. Bewildering in themselves, these features are further complicated by grammatical compressions such as missing connectives, elliptic conditionals, one part of speech serving for another, and a fondness for Carlylean word combinations that look more German or Greek than familiarly English. The vocabulary, on the other hand, is consciously simple, and what Yeats terms the 'impurities' (4) common in Victorian poetry—allusions, in Meredith's case, to politics, science and German folklore—are quite unspecific. The verse's cerebral challenge is related immediately to its own preoccupations.

Underlying the experimentalism is a move to realistic subject matter. Meredith was influenced by the contemporary French novel to consider 'life . . . worthy of the Muse' (5), and to examine the phenomenon of specifically modern love. In the same volume of 1862 he followed Browning in his monologues and narratives of everyday English life. The challenge he issues in the monitory distich heading the original *Modern Love* is not essentially an intellectual one, but to a more comprehensive understanding: 'This is not meat / For little people or for fools' (6). Overall, the impressive diversity of intricate metres and forms is itself, as in Browning and Hardy, a humanist assertion of the mind's creative versatility, its power to control and redefine a new version of experience.

The verse seldom gives a sense of deep integration: there is characteristically a conflict between formal definition and elusiveness of point. The mind usually wishes to delay and dwell while the verse beats on. *Modern Love*, for instance, so shockingly original in several ways, is after all framed in a highly shaped sonnet-sequence, however ironic the Petrarchan allusion is intended to be; and twenty five of the poems in the 1883 volume are in this uncompromising form. Only in the Miltonic 'Lucifer in Starlight' does the tautness seem directly expressive, acting out the restraint of 'unalterable law.' (7) His general insistence on metrical quantities, rhyming patterns and end-stopped lines provides the established structure against which he must register his significant effects.

The 'Ode to the Spirit of Earth in Autumn', with its conceptual dislocations, achieves in this way something of the authentic odic tension between rhapsody and formal dignity. The most memorable metrical experiments, as in the trochaic variations noted by Meredith in 'Love in the Valley', involve an intriguing compromise with strong stress metres, so that a single heavily stressed syllable can replace a whole foot, as in sprung rhythm:

/ /   /   /   /   /   /

Up lanes, woods through, they troop in joyful bands.

. . .

/   /   /   /   /   /   /

Large and smoky red the sun's cold disk drops. (8)

He is particularly sensitive to the mimetic potential of verse structure, as his defence of the blank octosyllabics of 'The South-West Wind in the Woodland' demonstrates:

> Nor could I find any other (better) mode of giving my impression of the reckless rushing rapidity, and sweeping sound of the great wind among the foliage which I felt impelled to do in such manner that the ear should only be conscious of swiftness, and no sweetness; and that there should be no direct pause throughout. This (in my mind) the hurrying measure of the four feet gives. (9)

The rhymed octosyllabics of 'The Lark Ascending' similarly act out the fluidity throughout the slight resistances of the bird's 'rounding' flight. A counterpoint is set up between the rhymes and the breathlessly extended sentences, as in the single sentence of sixty-four lines which makes up the opening verse-paragraph. In 'Dirge in Woods', the short lines detach themselves, as do the unfertilized cones, from the rhapsodic rush of life in the branches above: 'And we go,/ . . . /Even we, / Even so.' (10) Moments of such assured verse control can support the emotional cogency behind an argument, as in the claim that the bird's song in 'The Thrush in February' can heal the divide between life and death:

> Glimpse of its livingness will wave
> A light the senses can discern

>   Across the river of the death,
>   Their close. (11)

Meredith told Sidney Colvin that he worked for 'concentration and suggestion' (12), and the effect produced, though it owes something to these subtle formal tensions between expression and arrangement, is the result chiefly of his curious uses of imagery. The notorious metaphoric density is, in fact, a kind of excited positivism that, in Edward Thomas's account, 'help(s) the mind of the reader to transmutations (of matter)'. (13) Starting with real scenes, often from the Surrey woods, he generates philosophical allegories, as in 'Hymn to Colour' and 'The Woods of Westermain', or enormous symbols, such as the south west wind, dawn or sunset, by compounding a train of shifting images. The recalcitrance of the metaphorical items, which insist on their own disparateness, to the speedy urgency of their linking expresses the crucial creative tussle for Meredith—between the description of realist experience and the transforming meanings that the mind gives it. Though these meanings usually end up being explicitly abstracted, the rapidity of the mind's organizing activity can itself seem expressive of the natural life-force it is with difficulty eliciting from the fixed objects of natural perception. The impression, supported by Meredith's own account of the 'confusion' arising 'when strong emotion is in tide against the active mind' (14), is mostly of a mind struggling to formulate a rational upshot from the flow of powerful sensations. When the rapturous identification with nature occurs, it is typically conveyed in huge synæsthetic effects that overwhelm in their simultaneity any sense of separate, individually controlled response, but which are held together by the dominant Meredithian metaphor for the merging of natural experience and human creativity: the orchestral chord.

All Meredith's techniques of imagery have as their specific implication the relegation and possible transcendence of the sensational self. In this respect he has suffered badly from the wrong-headedness of more recent critics who have complained about the 'very disturbing anonymity of much of (his) verse' (15), and lamented his 'never quite achieving the authority of language which would have given a true self to his poetry.' (16) His central endeavour is precisely to create in natural objects symbols of the transcended self, like the ascending lark and the February thrush, instantly evolving the altruistic spirit from the sensationalist blood. So he deliberately avoids the lyrical 'I' in order 'to spread light when (his) proud letter I / Drops prone and void as any thoughtless dash.' (17) Success for him was, as he said, to become the adjective, 'Meredithian'. (18)

His complex effects of personification are representative. Human purposefulness may appear to be reflected in the natural context, but only to express the mind's active energies:

> Clouds—are they bony witches?—swarms,
> Darting swift on the robber's flight,
> Hurry an infant sky in arms. (19)

There is a naivety about incorrigibly human ways of seeing that has finally to concede the simple rightness of Earth:

> The lover of life holds life in his hand,
>   As the hills hold the day. (20)

The aim is finally to adopt the viewpoint of Earth herself—as at the end of 'The Thrush in February'; though usually, as there, it rests in the ultimate compromise of a benevolent maternal personification:

> We fall, or view our treasures fall,
> Unclouded, as beholds her flowers
>
> Earth, from a night of frosty wreck,
> Enrobed in morning's mounted fire,
> When lowly, with a broken neck,
> The crocus lays her cheek to mire. (21)

By withdrawing the subjective element in this way he is withdrawing the only point of perception that defines, for instance, the distinctness of night and day and life and death. In poems like 'In the Woods', where he is 'Between the two twilights' (22), and 'Night of Frost in May', that has the same ambivalent setting—'With splendour of a silver day, / A frosted night had opened May' (23)—the goal is to enter the natural continuum by will or imagination. Poems like 'Hymn to

16

Colour' and 'A Ballad of Past Meridian' affirm its achievement:

> Then memory, like the nightjar on the pine,
> And sightless hope, a woodlark in night sky,
> Joined notes of Death and Life till night's decline:
> Of Death, of Life, those inwound notes are mine. (24)

In 'Hymn to Colour' there is a gradual revelation of the world of nature that is always potentially there, and that grows into realization from out of the darkness: 'Death met I too, / And saw the dawn glow through.' (25) But the dawning of human potential in all objects of nature, when we can 'see in mould the rose unfold' (26), requires creative evocation. As Meredith's best recent commentator notes, 'the line between intensification and ornamentation is hard to draw.' (27) It is the border between imaginative investigation and the celebration of accomplished transcendence, with

> Reason herself, tiptoe
> At the ultimate bound of her wit
> On the verges of Night and Day. (28)

At such points the objects' potential for the creation of human value expresses itself in delicately ambiguous artifice: 'What busy bits of motioned wits / Through antlered mosswork strive.' (29) 'Night of Frost in May' is particularly precious in this way—in the appearance of metal and jewel worked by the impersonal agency of frost:

> The bud in jewelled grasp was nipped
> . . .
> A crystal off the green leaf slipped.
> . . .
> Endless the crossing multiplied
> Of silver and of gold string.
> . . .
> . . . how shook,
> Nigh speech of mouth, the sparkle-crest
> Seen spinning on the bracken-crook. (30)

This is the great poem—perhaps because it lies at the centre of Meredith's unresolved experimentalism. It dominates the succeeding twenty-year period of profitable novel-writing in which he wins through from the poem's working title of 'The Tragedy of Modern Love' to his final comic vision of society and the assured nature philosophy that complements it.

The volume of 1862 first reveals his familiarity with modern evolutionary theories, and in the course of this sequence the disastrous incongruity of Darwin and Petrarch, of ephemerae (1) clinging to ideals of courtly love, is shown up:

> Then if we study Nature we are wise.
> Thus do the few who live but with the day:
> The scientific animals are they.—
> Lady, this is my sonnet to your eyes. (2)

How can the 'May flies' (3) learn to live for the day? Anxiously, not without cynicism, the contemporary mind is shown trying to reorganize its cherished outlooks in the light of the new world-view:

> 'I play for Seasons; not Eternities'
> Says Nature, laughing on her way. 'So must
> All those whose stake is nothing more than dust!' (4)

In the first version of 'Love in the Valley', 1851, there had been no sense of division between his longing for the girl and the rich sensuousness of nature she both invests and is enveloped by. But by the second version of 1878, though girl and nature are again at one, the kind of love described is subtly different. There is in the later version the suggestion that the girl is 'sweeter unpossessed.' (5) The ambivalence of desire is at one point hinted at almost wistfully:

> Love that so desires would fain keep her changeless;
>   Fain would fling the net, and fain have her free. (6)

This later detachment touches on a complexity in the love poems from *Modern Love* onwards. The private pangs of sexual jealousy, and possibly an associated sense of inadequacy, lie behind the poem on the decline of his first marriage (though they are precisely disavowed in it, since there he leaves his wife's adultery open to question and invents a compensatory affair with a mistress.) They are relieved only by the gradual refutation of erotic love, which thereafter becomes combined with impulses of violence and death. An alternative evocation is suggested of philoprogenitiveness which transcends individual desire and promises a sense of inherent benevolence in the natural scheme:

> Love that had robbed us of immortal things,
> This little moment mercifully gave,
> Where I have seen across the twilight wave
> The swan sail with her young beneath her wings. (7)

After *Modern Love* the tragic vision continues in the love poetry of the *Ballads and Poems of Tragic Life*, 1887, where, in appropriately primitive settings, the coupling of Attila and Ildico ends in death and castration:

> Humped and grinning like a cat,
> Teeth for lips!—'tis she! she stares,
> Glittering through her bristled hairs (8)

and King Harald convulses to death, having struck down his adulterous wife and unborn child.

In *Modern Love*, the wife is unable to adapt. She insists on assuming that her husband maintains an erotic desire for his mistress (though in the course of the sequence he has consciously come to renounce it); and in a gesture of misplaced generosity she kills herself. If in so doing she enacts the fate of Eros, she also—and her suicide is another of Meredith's inventions: his wife died of natural causes—appeases in the husband a developing wish to have removed the object of a desire he either cannot or will not fulfil:

> Thus piteously Love closed what he begat:
> The union of this ever-diverse pair! (9)

Curiously, his sexual evasiveness is wrapped up in valuable insights. Moving towards what will become Meredith's matured philosophy of the need to transcend blood sensationalism by an altruistic self-dispersion into nature, the husband's tolerance deepens. In the context of a deliberately exploratory poem that leaves most of its conclusions open: 'Ah, what a dusty answer gets the soul / When hot for certainties in this our life!—' (10), he sees the certain fallacy of simple-minded moral categories when a man and a woman are honestly opposed:

> In tragic life, God wot,
> No villain need be! Passions spin the plot:
> We are betrayed by what is false within. (11)

Yet what he never comes to realize, not even when the husband turns into the supposedly detached persona of narrator at the end, but what is undeniable in the sensitive revelations of the poetry, is that the husband's idealistic urge to sexual evasiveness, to transcend sensationalism, is the key ingredient in their incompatibility, rather than a possible answer for them both. The poem finally leaves the impression of Meredith's having come closer to clarifying the basis of his own position—and there is some satisfaction in this—rather than having come to terms with the wife's very different personality. Nonetheless, the dramatization of the husband's morbid idealism is irrefutably there in the poem. His accusations are ironically self-revealing: his wife tries to 'tame' (12) him; she creates a domestic idyll to restrict his aspirations to social altruism (13); she wants to carry on living in a dream, so that his illusory rôle of 'fairy prince' will really be that of a puppet (14); his mistress similarly wants to make a mannikin out of him (15). The fact of her adultery is not essential: it is simply representative of the nature of a creature he sees as peculiarly embodying 'this agony of flesh!' (16) In a welter of maniacally melodramatic imagery accompanied by Biblical diction he conveys the moral repulsiveness of his attraction to this snake-like witch, who brings out in him the demon and the beast.

Emerging throughout, on the other hand, in recurrent images of sunset, sea and timelessness, is a conviction of emotional coherence that tells the reader more than either of the two official tellers. As the poem formally arranges itself around moments of intense affective turmoil, streams of diffuse but pervasive symbolism act out impersonal fluctuations of feeling that occasionally find resolution in images of natural integration. This reading of nature intimates the eventual benign transcendence of the urges of the sensational 'id' that continuously threatens to distort and destroy the possibility of assurance.

But as yet the human perception of a deep natural integration is mostly recalcitrant:

> Mark where the pressing wind shoots javelin-like,
> Its skeleton shadow on the broad-backed wave!
> Here is a fitting spot to dig Love's grave;
> Here where the ponderous breakers plunge and strike,
> And dart their hissing tongues high up the sand. (17)

Meredith does, however, suggest the provisional achievement of a new order of values, when the old disastrous attempt to preserve love's erotic heyday unchanged seems acceptably replaced by the rich stasis of a natural moment:

> We had not to look back on summer joys,
> Or forward to a summer of bright dye:
> . . .
> Love that had robbed us of immortal things,
> This little moment mercifully gave,
> And still I see across the twilight wave
> The swan sail with her young beneath her wings. (18)

The poem's overall finding is of a more powerful and honester agitation for human values than the Victorian novel ever matched. It registers the release of a confusion of blood and spirit, of sensationalist and self-surrendering passion—a confusion revealingly close to the idiosyncratic roots of Meredith's altruism:

> In tragic hints here see what evermore
> Moves dark as yonder midnight ocean's force,
> Thundering like ramping hosts of warrior horse,
> To throw that faint thin line upon the shore! (19)

V INFLUENCES

Hardy admitted Meredith's to the shadowy flock of unsubduable English voices: 'His words wing on—as live words will.' (1) This tribute is of peculiar interest since Hardy's overt thought could scarcely be more opposed to that of Meredith, who is the most resilient spokesman of the Wordsworthian-Goethean tradition that the natural conditions of our life are adequate to the formulation of a hopeful philosophy. Even if his creed is more genuinely experimental than his reputation usually suggests, so that he claims only, in relation to Hardy's work, 'I keep on the causeway between the bogs of optimism and pessimism' (2), the human values salvaged from the natural context by his English successors have been wrier and more problematic. Nevertheless those values often seem to me to owe something to Meredith. I think, for example, a poem like Hardy's 'The Darkling Thrush' weighs the implications of Meredith's claims in 'The Thrush in February', and that Edward Thomas's questioning surveys of silent nature in a poem like 'March' bring to mind Meredith's 'Night of Frost in May'.

Meredith's 'The Meeting' might almost have been written by Hardy, who, in poems like 'On the Way' or 'She Did Not Turn', is intrigued by the same theme of the potential encounter, either promised or denied, between individuals locked in private worlds. Hardy's technique of hinting at the impersonal undercurrents destroying the relationship between these worlds, when 'There is some hid dread afoot / That we cannot trace' (3), as in the arrival of sexual jealousy:

> He slid apart
> Who had thought her heart
> His own, and not aboard
> A bark, sea-bound . . . .
> That night they found
> Between them lay a sword (4)

—and the use of natural expressionism to convey the forces of domestic turmoil:

> Roaring high and roaring low was the sea
> Behind the headland shores:
> It symboled the slamming of doors,
> Or a regiment hurrying over hollow floors . . . .
> And there we two stood, hands clasped; I and she! (5)

—unmistakably recall *Modern Love*. The theme of marital disintegration in Meredith's masterpiece, and its overall strategy, doubtlessly affected by Tennyson's *In Memoriam*, of locating the crucial psychological moments that map out the course of a relationship, the mixture of intimacy and puzzlement when, as Meredith puts it, '(He) claim(s) a phantom-woman in the Past' (6), evidently influenced Hardy deeply. Robert Lowell also, as has been pointed out (7), with his revival of the sixteen-line stanza in 'The Mills of the Kavanaughs' alludes explictly to the combination of emotional complexity and formal restraint in Meredith's record of the fluctuations of a marriage. Lowell's poem dramatizes a wife's struggle decorously to preserve the memory of a tortured love for her husband, despite the covert horror of his having been shell-shocked into madness and violence at Pearl Harbour.

If in *Modern Love* Meredith developed structural effects from *In Memoriam* it was also necessary for him, in order to make his poetry work, to jettison Tennysonian diction which he came to associate with a lack of 'vital humanity' (8). He reacted from what Yeats terms the 'curious intricate rich-ness' (9) of his most successful early poem, 'Love in the Valley', to try his hand at the conversational oddities of the Browningesque monologue in poems like 'The Old Chartist', and, under the influence of the formless intensity exploited by the alternative school of 'spasmodic' poets and the Tennyson of *Maud*, he progressively formulated an idiosyncratic idiom as intellectually exercising as that of Browning or Donne (10). The shift was, as Lawrence points out (11), the Meredithian response to the need behind Synge's call for the brutalization of English poetry.

Eliot, who objected fundamentally to Meredith's radicalism, compares his experimentalism to that of Hopkins: 'they have similar tricks' (12). Occasionally the similarity is striking, as at the beginning of 'Hard Weather'. Both poets are attempting to elicit the impression of a natural dynamism. Whereas Eliot reckons Hopkins is a considerable poet because he has 'the dignity of the Church' behind his endeavours, not every reader will share his wish to discount Meredith for a secular enterprise that attempts to reconcile such leaders of modern thought as Goethe, Carlyle, Comte, Darwin and Mazzini. His undogmatic open-mindedness—he ridiculed 'The Parsonry' of Victorian sages like Ruskin (13)— produced experiments that others have found usable. Though his specific faith in evolu-tionary meliorism has passed out of fashion, the enthusiastic élan in such prose passages as the highly-charged description of the storm by night in the 'Nature Speaks' chapter of *The Ordeal of Richard Feverel* and related poems distinctly affected Lawrence's treatment of the physical rapport between man and nature (14). What Virginia Woolf refers to as Meredith's 'perpetual imagery' (15) was also an element in Joyce's interpretation of the 'stream of consciousness' technique in *Ulysses* (16).

Meredith has, of course, always been better known as a novelist, though he began and ended his writing career as a largely neglected poet, who lamented to a friend in old age: 'Only a few read my verse, and yet it is that for which I care most.' (17) It fits well with his theory of self-contribution to society that his poems were taken as a positive inspiration in living by the pre-First World War generation, and have proved so variously involving for other writers. That is exactly why Meredith wrote them—not to have them enshrined as admired artefacts. His dynamic largeness of assertion is the opposite of self-aggrandizing, as the lines engraved on his tombstone in Dorking Cemetery state:

> Our life is but a little holding, lent
> To do a mighty labour: we are one
> With heaven and the stars when it is spent
> To serve God's aim: else die we with the sun. (18)

Chesterton's account of a visit towards the end of Meredith's life wonderfully reveals the essence of his gift:

> He was deaf and he talked like a torrent—not about the books he had written—he was too much alive for that. He talked about the books he had not written. He asked me to write one of the stories for him, as he would have asked the milkman, if he had been talking to the milkman . . . . I went out of that garden with a blurred sensation of the million possibilities of creative literature. (19)

PRINCIPAL EDITIONS OF MEREDITH'S POETRY

CHECKLIST OF TITLES

Poems, London, 1851.

Modern Love and Poems of the English Roadside, with Poems and Ballads, London, 1862.

Poems and Lyrics of the Joy of Earth, London, 1883.

Ballads and Poems of Tragic Life, London and New York, 1887.

A Reading of Earth, London and New York, 1888.

Modern Love, A Reprint, to which is added the Sage Enamoured and the Honest Lady, London and New York, 1892.

Poems: The Empty Purse, with Odes to the Comic Spirit, To Youth in Memory, and Verses, London, 1892.

Selected Poems, London, 1897.

Odes in Contribution to the Song of French History, London, 1898.

Poems, in *The Works of George Meredith*, the 'De Luxe' Edition, ed. William Maxse Meredith, 36 vols., London, 1898-1912. XXIX—XXXI (the first three of four poetry volumes), 1898, supervised by the author.

A Reading of Life with Other Poems, London, 1901.

POSTHUMOUS EDITIONS

Last Poems, ed. W. M. Meredith, London, 1909.

Twenty Poems (from *Household Words*), ed. B. W. Matz, London, privately printed, 1909.

The 'De Luxe' Edition, XXXIII (the fourth poetry volume), 1910; XXXVI (*Bibliography and Various Readings*), 1911.

COLLECTED EDITIONS

The Poetical Works of George Meredith, with some notes by G. M. Trevelyan, London, 1912.

The Poems of George Meredith, ed. Phyllis B. Bartlett, 2 vols., New Haven and London, 1978.

Making the following selections, I have tried to represent the span and variety of a body of poetry published over almost sixty years. The poems included are intended overall to constitute Meredith's claim to be considered of lasting significance, as both a love and nature poet. But as well as containing the anthologist's nuggets this selection aims to show him in development and taking his political line in his own day.

I have been forced for lack of space ruefully to exclude several long poems which the interested reader should look up. I have left out, for instance, one of Meredith's best known-about poems, 'The Woods of Westermain', because I think it is too bare an exposition of his nature philosophy to warrant its full length. All the poems here printed are, as I think they should be, complete; otherwise I should have been tempted to print the two short opening sections of this poem. One of his most striking poems about love is 'The Nuptials of Attila'; but I have included rather the much shorter, in some ways similar, 'King Harald's Trance'. If I could have found room for any of the philosophical poems on mythological subjects, it would have been for 'The Day of the Daughter of Hades'.

The poems chosen are printed in the order of their first book publication. The only exception is 'Love in the Valley', which exists in two completely distinct versions. I print the second version in chronological sequence, and the original in an appendix. Dates of original separate publication of poems, and of composition when known, are given in the notes. Line numeration is editorial.

The texts are the last printed in the author's lifetime; except, of course, for those of poems left unpublished. For all poems published before 1898, they are those of the first three volumes of the 'De Luxe' edition of that year, supervised by Meredith. The text of 'Song in the Songless' is that of *A Reading of Life*, 1901; and those of 'The Fair Bedfellow' and 'Aimée' are taken from Phyllis B. Bartlett's edition, *The Poems of George Meredith*, where they first appeared in 1978. 'In the Woods' has an extremely complicated textual history. Since the form in which I print it is that which first appeared in G. M. Trevelyan's *The Poetical Works*, 1912, I group it with the Poems Left Unpublished.

Much of Meredith's poetry is fascinatingly obscure. The interpretations I offer the reader in the notes are naturally tentative, and are intended simply to give him or her the confidence of seeing someone else's attempts.

I hope the Selected Bibiliography at the end will help anyone wishing to follow up points raised in my introduction to develop an interest in Meredith's neglected poetry.

from **POEMS (1851)**

SONG
Spring

When buds of palm do burst and spread
    Their downy feathers in the lane,
And orchard blossoms, white and red,
    Breathe Spring delight for Autumn gain;
    And the skylark shakes his wings in the rain;

O then is the season to look for a bride!
    Choose her warily, woo her unseen;
For the choicest maids are those that hide
    Like dewy violets under the green.

from **MODERN LOVE AND POEMS OF THE ENGLISH ROADSIDE (1862)**

THE MEETING

The old coach-road through a common of furze,
    With knolls of pine ran white;
Berries of autumn, with thistles, and burrs,
    And spider-threads, droop'd in the light.

The light in a thin blue veil peered sick;
    The sheep grazed close and still;
The smoke of a farm by a yellow rick
    Curled lazily under a hill.

No fly shook the round of the silver net;
    No insect the swift bird chased;   10
Only two travellers moved and met
    Across that hazy waste.

One was a girl with a babe that throve,
    Her ruin and her bliss;
One was a youth with a lawless love,
    Who clasped it the more for this.

The girl for her babe hummed prayerful speech;
    The youth for his love did pray;
Each cast a wistful look on each,
    And either went their way.   20

THE PROMISE IN DISTURBANCE

How low when angels fall their black descent,
Our primal thunder tells: known is the pain
Of music, that nigh throning wisdom went,
And one false note cast wailful to the insane.
Now seems the language heard of Love as rain
To make a mire where fruitfulness was meant.
The golden harp gives out a jangled strain,
Too like revolt from heaven's Omnipotent.
But listen in the thought; so may there come
Conception of a newly-added chord,
Commanding space beyond where ear has home.
In labour of the trouble at its fount,
Leads Life to an intelligible Lord
The rebel discords up the sacred mount.

MODERN LOVE

I   By this he knew she wept with waking eyes:
That, at his hand's light quiver by her head,
The strange low sobs that shook their common bed,
Were called into her with a sharp surprise,
And strangled mute, like little gaping snakes,
Dreadfully venomous to him. She lay
Stone-still, and the long darkness flowed away
With muffled pulses. Then, as midnight makes
Her giant heart of Memory and Tears
Drink the pale drug of silence, and so beat
Sleep's heavy measure, they from head to feet
Were moveless, looking through their dead black years,
By vain regret scrawled over the blank wall.
Like sculptured effigies they might be seen
Upon their marriage-tomb, the sword between;
Each wishing for the sword that severs all.

II   It ended, and the morrow brought the task.
      Her eyes were guilty gates, that let him in
      By shutting all too zealous for their sin:
      Each sucked a secret, and each wore a mask.
      But, oh, the bitter taste her beauty had!
      He sickened as at breath of poison-flowers:
      A languid humour stole among the hours,
      And if their smiles encountered, he went mad,
      And raged deep inward, till the light was brown
      Before his vision, and the world forgot,
      Looked wicked as some old dull murder-spot.
      A star with lurid beams, she seemed to crown
      The pit of infamy: and then again
      He fainted on his vengefulness, and strove
      To ape the magnanimity of love,
      And smote himself, a shuddering heap of pain.

III   This was the woman; what now of the man?
      But pass him. If he comes beneath a heel,
      He shall be crushed until he cannot feel,
      Or, being callous, haply till he can.
      But he is nothing:—nothing? Only mark
      The rich light striking out from her on him!
      Ha! what a sense it is when her eyes swim
      Across the man she singles, leaving dark
      All else! Lord God, who mad'st the thing so fair,
      See that I am drawn to her even now!
      It cannot be such harm on her cool brow
      To put a kiss? Yet if I meet him there!
      But she is mine! Ah, no! I know too well
      I claim a star whose light is overcast:
      I claim a phantom-woman in the Past.
      The hour has struck, though I heard not the bell!

IV   All other joys of life he strove to warm,
      And magnify, and catch them to his lip:
      But they had suffered shipwreck with the ship,
      And gazed upon him sallow from the storm.
      Or if Delusion came, 'twas but to show
      The coming minute mock the one that went.
      Cold as a mountain in its star-pitched tent,

Stood high Philosophy, less friend than foe:
Whom self-caged Passion, from its prison-bars,
Is always watching with a wondering hate.
Not till the fire is dying in the grate,
Look we for any kinship with the stars.
Oh, wisdom never comes when it is gold,
And the great price we pay for it full worth:
We have it only when we are half earth.
Little avails that coinage to the old!

V   A message from her set his brain aflame.
A world of household matters filled her mind,
Wherein he saw hypocrisy designed:
She treated him as something that is tame,
And but at other provocation bites.
Familiar was her shoulder in the glass,
Through that dark rain: yet it may come to pass
That a changed eye finds such familiar sights
More keenly tempting than new loveliness.
The 'What has been' a moment seemed his own:
The splendours, mysteries, dearer because known,
Nor less divine: Love's inmost sacredness,
Called to him, 'Come!'—In his restraining start,
Eyes nurtured to be looked at, scarce could see
A wave of the great waves of Destiny
Convulsed at a checked impulse of the heart.

VI   It chanced his lips did meet her forehead cool.
She had no blush, but slanted down her eye.
Shamed nature, then, confesses love can die:
And most she punishes the tender fool
Who will believe what honours her the most!
Dead! is it dead? She has a pulse, and flow
Of tears, the price of blood-drops, as I know,
For whom the midnight sobs around Love's ghost,
Since then I heard her, and so will sob on.
The love is here; it has but changed its aim.
O bitter barren woman! what's the name?
The name, the name, the new name thou hast won?
Behold me striking the world's coward stroke!
That will I not do, though the sting is dire.

　　　　　—Beneath the surface this, while by the fire
　　　　　They sat, she laughing at a quiet joke.

VII　　She issues radiant from her dressing-room,
　　　　　Like one prepared to scale an upper sphere:
　　　　　—By stirring up a lower, much I fear!
　　　　　How deftly that oiled barber lays his bloom!
　　　　　That long-shanked dapper Cupid with frisked curls,
　　　　　Can make known women torturingly fair;
　　　　　The gold-eyed serpent dwelling in rich hair,
　　　　　Awakes beneath his magic whisks and twirls.
　　　　　His art can take the eyes from out my head,
　　　　　Until I see with eyes of other men;
　　　　　While deeper knowledge crouches in its den,
　　　　　And sends a spark up:—is it true we are wed?
　　　　　Yea! filthiness of body is most vile,
　　　　　But faithlessness of heart I do hold worse.
　　　　　The former, it were not so great a curse
　　　　　To read on the steel-mirror of her smile.

VIII　Yet it was plain she struggled, and that salt
　　　　　Of righteous feeling made her pitiful.
　　　　　Poor twisting worm, so queenly beautiful!
　　　　　Where came the cleft between us? whose the fault?
　　　　　My tears are on thee, that have rarely dropped
　　　　　As balm for any bitter wound of mine:
　　　　　My breast will open for thee at a sign!
　　　　　But, no: we are two reed-pipes, coarsely stopped:
　　　　　The God once filled them with his mellow breath;
　　　　　And they were music till he flung them down,
　　　　　Used! used! Hear now the discord-loving clown
　　　　　Puff his gross spirit in them, worse than death!
　　　　　I do not know myself without thee more:
　　　　　In this unholy battle I grow base:
　　　　　If the same soul be under the same face,
　　　　　Speak, and a taste of that old time restore!

IX　　He felt the wild beast in him betweenwhiles
　　　　　So masterfully rude, that he would grieve
　　　　　To see the helpless delicate thing receive
　　　　　His guardianship through certain dark defiles.

Had he not teeth to rend, and hunger too?
But still he spared her. Once: 'Have you no fear?'
He said: 'twas dusk; she in his grasp; none near.
She laughed: 'No, surely; am I not with you?'
And uttering that soft starry 'you', she leaned
Her gentle body near him, looking up;
And from her eyes, as from a poison-cup,
He drank until the flittering eyelids screened.
Devilish malignant witch! and oh, young beam
Of heaven's circle-glory! Here thy shape
To squeeze like an intoxicating grape—
I might, and yet thou goest safe, supreme.

X   But where began the change; and what's my crime?
       The wretch condemned, who has not been arraigned,
       Chafes at his sentence. Shall I, unsustained,
       Drag on Love's nerveless body thro' all time?
       I must have slept, since now I wake. Prepare,
       You lovers, to know Love a thing of moods:
       Not like hard life, of laws. In Love's deep woods,
       I dreamt of loyal Life:—the offence is there!
       Love's jealous woods about the sun are curled;
       At least, the sun far brighter there did beam.—
       My crime is, that the puppet of a dream,
       I plotted to be worthy of the world.
       Oh, had I with my darling helped to mince
       The facts of life, you still had seen me go
       With hindward feather and with forward toe,
       Her much-adored delightful Fairy Prince!

XI   Out in the yellow meadows, where the bee
       Hums by us with the honey of the Spring,
       And showers of sweet notes from the larks on wing,
       Are dropping like a noon-dew, wander we.
       Or is it now? or was it then? for now,
       As then, the larks from running rings pour showers:
       The golden foot of May is on the flowers,
       And friendly shadows dance upon her brow.
       What's this, when Nature swears there is no change
       To challenge eyesight? Now, as then, the grace
       Of heaven seems holding earth in its embrace.

Nor eyes, nor heart, has she to feel it strange?
Look, woman, in the West. There wilt thou see
An amber cradle near the sun's decline:
Within it, featured even in death divine,
Is lying a dead infant, slain by thee.

XII   Not solely that the Future she destroys,
And the fair life which in the distance lies
For all men, beckoning out from dim rich skies:
Nor that the passing hour's supporting joys
Have lost the keen-edged flavour, which begat
Distinction in old times, and still should breed
Sweet Memory, and Hope,—earth's modest seed,
And heaven's high-prompting: not that the world is flat
Since that soft-luring creature I embraced,
Among the children of Illusion went:
Methinks with all this loss I were content,
If the mad Past, on which my foot is based,
Were firm, or might be blotted: but the whole
Of life is mixed: the mocking Past will stay:
And if I drink oblivion of a day,
So shorten I the stature of my soul.

XIII   'I play for Seasons; not Eternities!'
Says Nature, laughing on her way. 'So must
All those whose stake is nothing more than dust!'
And lo, she wins, and of her harmonies
She is full sure! Upon her dying rose,
She drops a look of fondness, and goes by,
Scarce any retrospection in her eye;
For she the laws of growth most deeply knows,
Whose hands bear, here, a seed-bag—there, an urn.
Pledged she herself to aught, 'twould mark her end!
This lesson of our only visible friend,
Can we not teach our foolish hearts to learn?
Yes! yes!—but, oh, our human rose is fair
Surpassingly! Lose calmly Love's great bliss,
When the renewed for ever of a kiss
Whirls life within the shower of loosened hair!

XIV   What soul would bargain for a cure that brings
          Contempt the nobler agony to kill?
          Rather let me bear on the bitter ill,
          And strike this rusty bosom with new stings!
          It seems there is another veering fit,
          Since on a gold-haired lady's eyeballs pure,
          I looked with little prospect of a cure,
          The while her mouth's red bow loosed shafts of wit.
          Just heaven! can it be true that jealousy
          Has decked the woman thus? and does her head
          Swim somewhat for possessions forfeited?
          Madam, you teach me many things that be.
          I open an old book, and there I find,
          That 'Women still may love whom they deceive.'
          Such love I prize not, madam: by your leave,
          The game you play at is not to my mind.

XV   I think she sleeps: it must be sleep, when low
          Hangs that abandoned arm toward the floor;
          The face turned with it. Now make fast the door.
          Sleep on: it is your husband, not your foe.
          The Poet's black stage-lion of wronged love,
          Frights not our modern dames:—well if he did!
          Now will I pour new light upon that lid,
          Full-sloping like the breasts beneath. 'Sweet dove,
          Your sleep is pure. Nay, pardon: I disturb.
          I do not? good!' Her waking infant-stare
          Grows woman to the burden my hands bear:
          Her own handwriting to me when no curb
          Was left on Passion's tongue. She trembles through;
          A woman's tremble—the whole instrument:—
          I show another letter lately sent.
          The words are very like: the name is new.

XVI   In our old shipwrecked days there was an hour,
          When in the firelight steadily aglow,
          Joined slackly, we beheld the red chasm grow
          Among the clicking coals. Our library-bower
          That eve was left to us: and hushed we sat
          As lovers to whom Time is whispering.
          From sudden-opened doors we heard them sing:

The nodding elders mixed good wine with chat.
Well knew we that Life's greatest treasure lay
With us, and of it was our talk. 'Ah, yes!
Love dies!' I said: I never thought it less.
She yearned to me that sentence to unsay.
Then when the fire domed blackening, I found
Her cheek was salt against my kiss, and swift
Up the sharp scale of sobs her breast did lift:—
Now am I haunted by that taste! that sound!

XVII At dinner, she is hostess, I am host.
Went the feast ever cheerfuller? She keeps
The Topic over intellectual deeps
In buoyancy afloat. They see no ghost.
With sparkling surface-eyes we ply the ball:
It is in truth a most contagious game:
HIDING THE SKELETON, shall be its name.
Such play as this, the devils might appal!
But here's the greater wonder; in that we
Enamoured of an acting nought can tire,
Each other, like true hypocrites, admire;
Warm-lighted looks, Love's ephemerioe,
Shoot gaily o'er the dishes and the wine.
We waken envy of our happy lot.
Fast, sweet, and golden, shows the marriage-knot.
Dear guests, you now have seen Love's corpse-light shine.

XVIII Here Jack and Tom are paired with Moll and Meg.
Curved open to the river-reach is seen
A country merry-making on the green.
Fair space for signal shakings of the leg.
That little screwy fiddler from his booth,
Whence flows one nut-brown stream, commands the
    joints
Of all who caper here at various points.
I have known rustic revels in my youth:
The May-fly pleasures of a mind at ease.
An early goddess was a country lass:
A charmed Amphion-oak she tripped the grass.
What life was that I lived? The life of these?
Heaven keep them happy! Nature they seem near.

They must, I think, be wiser than I am;
They have the secret of the bull and lamb.
'Tis true that when we trace its source, 'tis beer.

XIX   No state is enviable. To the luck alone
Of some few favoured men I would put claim.
I bleed, but her who wounds I will not blame.
Have I not felt her heart as 'twere my own
Beat thro' me? could I hurt her? heaven and hell!
But I could hurt her cruelly! Can I let
My love's old time-piece to another set,
Swear it can't stop, and must for ever swell?
Sure, that's one way Love drifts into the mart
Where goat-legged buyers throng. I see not plain:—
My meaning is, it must not be again.
Great God! the maddest gambler throws his heart.
If any state be enviable on earth,
'Tis yon born idiot's, who, as days go by,
Still rubs his hands before him, like a fly,
In a queer sort of meditative mirth.

XX   I am not of those miserable males
Who sniff at vice and, daring not to snap,
Do therefore hope for heaven. I take the hap
Of all my deeds. The wind that fills my sails,
Propels; but I am helmsman. Am I wrecked,
I know the devil has sufficient weight
To bear: I lay it not on him, or fate.
Besides, he's damned. That man I do suspect
A coward, who would burden the poor deuce
With what ensues from his own slipperiness.
I have just found a wanton-scented tress
In an old desk, dusty for lack of use.
Of days and nights it is demonstrative,
That, like some aged star, gleam luridly.
If for those times I must ask charity,
Have I not any charity to give?

XXI   We three are on the cedar-shadowed lawn;
My friend being third. He who at love once laughed,
Is in the weak rib by a fatal shaft

38

Struck through, and tells his passion's bashful dawn
And radiant culmination, glorious crown,
When 'this' she said: went 'thus': most wondrous she.
Our eyes grow white, encountering: that we are three,
Forgetful; then together we look down.
But he demands our blessing; is convinced
That words of wedded lovers must bring good.
We question; if we dare! or if we should!
And pat him, with light laugh. We have not winced.
Next, she has fallen. Fainting points the sign
To happy things in wedlock. When she wakes,
She looks the star that thro' the cedar shakes:
Her lost moist hand clings mortally to mine.

XXII What may the woman labour to confess?
There is about her mouth a nervous twitch.
'Tis something to be told, or hidden:—which?
I get a glimpse of hell in this mild guess.
She has desires of touch, as if to feel
That all the household things are things she knew.
She stops before the glass. What sight in view?
A face that seems the latest to reveal!
For she turns from it hastily, and tossed
Irresolute, steals shadow-like to where
I stand; and wavering pale before me there,
Her tears fall still as oak-leaves after frost.
She will not speak. I will not ask. We are
League-sundered by the silent gulf between.
You burly lovers on the village green,
Yours is a lower, and a happier star!

XXIII 'Tis Christmas weather, and a country house
Receives us: rooms are full: we can but get
An attic-crib. Such lovers will not fret
At that, it is half-said. The great carouse
Knocks hard upon the midnight's hollow door,
But when I knock at hers, I see the pit.
Why did I come here in that dullard fit?
I enter, and lie couched upon the floor.
Passing, I caught the coverlet's quick beat:—
Come, Shame, burn to my soul! and Pride, and Pain—

Foul demons that have tortured me, enchain!
Out in the freezing darkness the lambs bleat.
The small bird stiffens in the low starlight.
I know not how, but shuddering as I slept,
I dreamed a banished angel to me crept:
My feet were nourished on her breasts all night.

XXIV The misery is greater, as I live!
To know her flesh so pure, so keen her sense,
That she does penance now for no offence,
Save against Love. The less can I forgive!
The less can I forgive, though I adore
That cruel lovely pallor which surrounds
Her footsteps; and the low vibrating sounds
That come on me, as from a magic shore.
Low are they, but most subtle to find out
The shrinking soul. Madam, 'tis understood
When women play upon their womanhood;
It means, a Season gone. And yet I doubt
But I am duped. That nun-like look waylays
My fancy. Oh! I do but wait a sign!
Pluck out the eyes of pride! thy mouth to mine!
Never! though I die thirsting. Go thy ways!

XXV You like not that French novel? Tell me why.
You think it quite unnatural. Let us see.
The actors are, it seems, the usual three:
Husband, and wife, and lover. She—but fie!
In England we'll not hear of it. Edmond,
The lover, her devout chagrin doth share;
Blanc-mange and absinthe are his penitent fare,
Till his pale aspect makes her over-fond:
So, to preclude fresh sin, he tries rosbif.
Meantime the husband is no more abused:
Auguste forgives her ere the tear is used.
Then hangeth all on one tremednous IF :—
If she will choose between them. She does choose;
And takes her husband, like a proper wife.
Unnatural? My dear, these things are life:
And life, some think, is worthy of the Muse.

XXVI   Love ere he bleeds, an eagle in high skies,
Has earth beneath his wings: from reddened eve
He views the rosy dawn. In vain they weave
The fatal web below while far he flies.
But when the arrow strikes him, there's a change.
He moves but in the track of his spent pain,
Whose red drops are the links of a harsh chain,
Binding him to the ground, with narrow range.
A subtle serpent then has Love become.
I had the eagle in my bosom erst:
Henceforward with the serpent I am cursed.
I can interpret where the mouth is dumb.
Speak, and I see the side-lie of a truth.
Perchance my heart may pardon you this deed:
But be no coward:—you that made Love bleed,
You must bear all the venom of his tooth!

XXVII   Distraction is the panacea, Sir!
I hear my oracle of Medicine say.
Doctor! that same specific yesterday
I tried, and the result will not deter
A second trial. Is the devil's line
Of golden hair, or raven black, composed?
And does a cheek, like any sea-shell rosed,
Or clear as widowed sky, seem most divine?
No matter, so I taste forgetfulness.
And if the devil snare me, body and mind,
Here gratefully I score:— he seeméd kind,
When not a soul would comfort my distress!
O sweet new world, in which I rise new made!
O Lady, once I gave love: now I take!
Lady, I must be flattered. Shouldst thou wake
The passion of a demon, be not afraid.

XXVIII   I must be flattered. The imperious
Desire speaks out. Lady, I am content
To play with you the game of Sentiment,
And with you enter on paths perilous;
But if across your beauty I throw light,
To make it threefold, it must be all mine.
First secret; then avowed. For I must shine

Envied,—I, lessened in my proper sight!
Be watchful of your beauty, Lady dear!
How much hangs on that lamp you cannot tell.
Most earnestly I pray you, tend it well:
And men shall see me as a burning sphere;
And men shall mark you eyeing me, and groan
To be the God of such a grand sunflower!
I feel the promptings of Satanic power,
While you do homage unto me alone.

XXIX   Am I failing? For no longer can I cast
A glory round about this head of gold.
Glory she wears, but springing from the mould;
Not like the consecration of the Past!
Is my soul beggared? Something more than earth
I cry for still: I cannot be at peace
In having Love upon a mortal lease.
I cannot take the woman at her worth!
Where is the ancient wealth wherewith I clothed
Our human nakedness, and could endow
With spiritual splendour a white brow
That else had grinned at me the fact I loathed?
A kiss is but a kiss now! and no wave
Of a great flood that whirls me to the sea.
But, as you will! we'll sit contentedly,
And eat our pot of honey on the grave.

XXX   What are we first? First, animals; and next
Intelligences at a leap; on whom
Pale lies the distant shadow of the tomb,
And all that draweth on the tomb for text.
Into which state comes Love, the crowning sun:
Beneath whose light the shadow loses form.
We are the lords of life, and life is warm.
Intelligence and instinct now are one.
But Nature says: 'My children most they seem
When they least know me: therefore I decree
That they shall suffer.' Swift doth young Love flee,
And we stand wakened, shivering from our dream.
Then if we study Nature we are wise.
Thus do the few who live but with the day:

The scientific animals are they.—
Lady, this is my sonnet to your eyes.

XXXI This golden head has wit in it. I live
Again, and a far higher life, near her.
Some women like a young philosopher;
Perchance because he is diminutive.
For woman's manly god must not exceed
Proportions of the natural nursing size.
Great poets and great sages draw no prize
With women: but the little lap-dog breed,
Who can be hugged, or on a mantel-piece
Perched up for adoration, these obtain
Her homage. And of this we men are vain?
Of this! 'Tis ordered for the world's increase!
Small flattery! Yet she has that rare gift
To beauty, Common Sense. I am approved.
It is not half so nice as being loved,
And yet I do prefer it. What's my drift?

XXXII Full faith I have she holds that rarest gift
To beauty, Common Sense. To see her lie
With her fair visage an inverted sky
Bloom-covered, while the underlids uplift,
Would almost wreck the faith; but when her mouth
(Can it kiss sweetly? sweetly!) would address
The inner me that thirsts for her no less,
And has so long been languishing in drouth,
I feel that I am matched; that I am man!
One restless corner of my heart or head,
That holds a dying something never dead,
Still frets, though Nature giveth all she can.
It means, that woman is not, I opine,
Her sex's antidote. Who seeks the asp
For serpents' bites? 'Twould calm me could I clasp
Shrieking Bacchantes with their souls of wine!

XXXIII 'In Paris, at the Louvre, there have I seen
The sumptuously-feathered angel pierce
Prone Lucifer, descending. Looked he fierce,
Showing the fight a fair one? Too serene!

The young Pharsalians did not disarray
Less willingly their locks of floating silk:
That suckling mouth of his, upon the milk
Of heaven might still be feasting through the fray.
Oh, Raphael! when men the Fiend do fight,
They conquer not upon such easy terms.
Half serpent in the struggle grow these worms.
And does he grow half human, all is right.'
This to my Lady in a distant spot,
Upon the theme: *While mind is mastering clay,*
Gross clay invades it. If the spy you play,
My wife, read this! Strange love talk, is it not?

XXXIV Madam would speak with me. So, now it comes:
The Deluge or else Fire! She's well; she thanks
My husbandship. Our chain on silence clanks.
Time leers between, above his twiddling thumbs.
Am I quite well? Most excellent in health!
The journals, too, I diligently peruse.
Vesuvius is expected to give news:
Niagara is no noisier. By stealth
Our eyes dart scrutinizing snakes. She's glad
I'm happy, says her quivering upper-lip.
'And are not you?' 'How can I be?' 'Take ship!
For happiness is somewhere to be had.'
'Nowhere for me!' Her voice is barely heard.
I am not melted, and make no pretence.
With commonplace I freeze her, tongue and sense.
Niagara or Vesuvius is deferred.

XXXV It is no vulgar nature I have wived.
Secretive, sensitive, she takes a wound
Deep to her soul, as if the sense had swooned,
And not a thought of vengeance had survived.
No confidences has she: but relief
Must come to one whose suffering is acute.
O have a care of natures that are mute!
They punish you in acts: their steps are brief.
What is she doing? What does she demand
From Providence or me? She is not one
Long to endure this torpidly, and shun

The drugs that crowd about a woman's hand.
At Forfeits during snow we played, and I
Must kiss her. 'Well performed!' I said: then she:
' 'Tis hardly worth the money, you agree?'
Save her? What for? To act this wedded lie!

XXXVI My Lady unto Madam makes her bow.
The charm of women is, that even while
You're probed by them for tears, you yet may smile,
Nay, laugh outright, as I have done just now.
The interview was gracious: they anoint
(To me aside) each other with fine praise:
Discriminating compliments they raise,
That hit with wondrous aim on the weak point:
My Lady's nose of Nature might complain.
It is not fashioned aptly to express
Her character of large-browed steadfastness.
But Madam says: Thereof she may be vain!
Now, Madam's faulty feature is a glazed
And inaccessible eye, that has soft fires,
Wide gates, at love-time only. This admires
My Lady. At the two I stand amazed.

XXXVII Along the garden terrace, under which
A purple valley (lighted at its edge
By smoky torch-flame on the long cloud-ledge
Whereunder dropped the chariot), glimmers rich,
A quiet company we pace, and wait
The dinner-bell in prae-digestive calm.
So sweet up violet banks the Southern balm
Breathes round, we care not if the bell be late:
Though here and there grey seniors question Time
In irritable coughings. With slow foot
The low rosed moon, the face of Music mute,
Begins among her silent bars to climb.
As in and out, in silvery dusk, we thread,
I hear the laugh of Madam, and discern
My Lady's heel before me at each turn.
Our tragedy, is it alive or dead?

XXXVIII Give to imagination some pure light
         In human form to fix it, or you shame
         The devils with that hideous human game:—
         Imagination urging appetite!
         Thus fallen have earth's greatest Gogmagogs,
         Who dazzle us, whom we can not revere:
         Imagination is the charioteer
         That, in default of better, drives the hogs.
         So, therefore, my dear Lady, let me love!
         My soul is arrowy to the light in you.
         You know me that I never can renew
         The bond that woman broke: what would you have?
         'Tis Love, or Vileness! not a choice between,
         Save petrifaction! What does Pity here?
         She killed a thing, and now it's dead, 'tis dear.
         Oh, when you counsel me, think what you mean!

XXXIX   She yields: my Lady in her noblest mood
         Has yielded: she, my golden-crownëd rose!
         The bride of every sense! more sweet than those
         Who breathe the violet breath of maidenhood.
         O visage of still music in the sky!
         Soft moon! I feel thy song, my fairest friend!
         True harmony within can apprehend
         Dumb harmony without. And hark! 'tis nigh!
         Belief has struck the note of sound: a gleam
         Of living silver shows me where she shook
         Her long white fingers down the shadowy brook,
         That sings her song, half-waking, half in dream.
         What two come here to mar this heavenly tune?
         A man is one: the woman bears my name,
         And honour. Their hands touch! Am I still tame?
         God, what a dancing spectre seems the moon!

XL   I bade my Lady think what she might mean.
         Know I my meaning, I? Can I love one,
         And yet be jealous of another? None
         Commits such folly. Terrible Love, I ween,
         Has might, even dead, half sighing to upheave
         The lightless seas of selfishness amain:
         Seas that in a man's heart have no rain

To fall and still them. Peace can I achieve,
By turning to this fountain-source of woe,
This woman, who's to Love as fire to wood?
She breathed the violet breath of maidenhood
Against my kisses once! but I say, No!
The thing is mocked at! Helplessly afloat,
I know not what I do, whereto I strive,
The dread that my old love may be alive,
Has seized my nursling new love by the throat.

XLI   How many a thing which we cast to the ground,
When others pick it up becomes a gem!
We grasp at all the wealth it is to them;
And by reflected light its worth is found.
Yet for us still 'tis nothing! and that zeal
Of false appreciation quickly fades.
This truth is little known to human shades,
How rare from their own instinct 'tis to feel!
They waste the soul with spurious desire,
That is not the ripe flame upon the bough.
We two have taken up a lifeless vow
To rob a living passion: dust for fire!
Madam is grave, and eyes the clock that tells
Approaching midnight. We have struck despair
Into two hearts. O, look we like a pair
Who for fresh nuptials joyfully yield all else?

XLII   I am to follow her. There is much grace
In women when thus bent on martyrdom.
They think that dignity of soul may come,
Perchance, with dignity of body. Base!
But I was taken by that air of cold
And statuesque sedateness, when she said
'I'm going'; lit a taper, bowed her head,
And went, as with the stride of Pallas bold.
Fleshly indifference horrible! The hands
Of Time now signal: O, she's safe from me!
Within those secret walls what do I see?
Where first she set the taper down she stands:
Not Pallas: Hebe shamed! Thoughts black as death,
Like a stirred pool in sunshine break. Her wrists

I catch: she faltering, as she half resists,
'You love . . . ? love . . . ? love . . . ?' all on an indrawn
    breath.

XLIII   Mark where the pressing wind shoots javelin-like,
    Its skeleton shadow on the broad-backed wave!
    Here is a fitting spot to dig Love's grave;
    Here where the ponderous breakers plunge and strike,
    And dart their hissing tongues high up the sand:
    In hearing of the ocean, and in sight
    Of those ribbed wind-streaks running into white.
    If I the death of Love had deeply planned,
    I never could have made it half so sure,
    As by the unblest kisses which upbraid
    The full-waked sense; or failing that, degrade!
    'Tis morning: but no morning can restore
    What we have forfeited. I see no sin:
    The wrong is mixed. In tragic life, God wot,
    No villain need be! Passions spin the plot:
    We are betrayed by what is false within.

XLIV   They say, that Pity in Love's service dwells,
    A porter at the rosy temple's gate.
    I missed him going: but it is my fate
    To come upon him now beside his wells;
    Whereby I know that I Love's temple leave,
    And that the purple doors have closed behind.
    Poor soul! if in those early days unkind,
    Thy power to sting had been but power to grieve,
    We now might with an equal spirit meet,
    And not be matched like innocence and vice.
    She for the Temple's worship has paid price,
    And takes the coin of Pity as a cheat.
    She sees through simulation to the bone:
    What's best in her impels her to the worst:
    Never, she cries, shall Pity soothe Love's thirst,
    Or foul hypocrisy for truth atone!

XLV   It is the season of the sweet wild rose,
    My Lady's emblem in the heart of me!
    So golden-crownëd shines she gloriously,

And with that softest dream of blood she glows:
Mild as an evening heaven round Hesper bright!
I pluck the flower, and smell it, and revive
The time when in her eyes I stood alive.
I seem to look upon it out of Night.
Here's Madam, stepping hastily. Her whims
Bid her demand the flower, which I let drop.
As I proceed, I feel her sharply stop,
And crush it under heel with trembling limbs.
She joins me in a cat-like way, and talks
Of company, and even condescends
To utter laughing scandal of old friends.
These are the summer days, and these our walks.

XLVI   At last we parley: we so strangely dumb
In such a close communion! It befell
About the sounding of the Matin-bell,
And lo! her place was vacant, and the hum
Of loneliness was round me. Then I rose,
And my disordered brain did guide my foot
To that old wood where our first love-salute
Was interchanged: the source of many throes!
There did I see her, not alone. I moved
Toward her, and made proffer of my arm.
She took it simply, with no rude alarm;
And that disturbing shadow passed reproved.
I felt the pained speech coming, and declared
My firm belief in her, ere she could speak.
A ghastly morning came into her cheek,
While with a widening soul on me she stared.

XLVII We saw the swallows gathering in the sky,
And in the osier-isle we heard them noise.
We had not to look back on summer joys,
Or forward to a summer of bright dye:
But in the largeness of the evening earth
Our spirits grew as we went side by side.
The hour became her husband and my bride.
Love that had robbed us so, thus blessed our dearth!
The pilgrims of the year waxed very loud
In multitudinous chatterings, as the flood

Full brown came from the West, and like pale blood
Expanded to the upper crimson cloud.
Love that had robbed us of immortal things,
This little moment mercifully gave,
Where I have seen across the twilight wave
The swan sail with her young beneath her wings.

XLVIII   Their sense is with their senses all mixed in,
Destroyed by subtleties these women are!
More brain, O Lord, more brain! or we shall mar
Utterly this fair garden we might win.
Behold! I looked for peace, and thought it near.
Our inmost hearts had opened, each to each.
We drank the pure daylight of honest speech.
Alas! that was the fatal draught, I fear.
For when of my lost Lady came the word,
This woman, O this agony of flesh!
Jealous devotion bade her break the mesh,
That I might seek that other like a bird.
I do adore the nobleness! despise
The act! She has gone forth, I know not where.
Will the hard world my sentience of her share?
I feel the truth; so let the world surmise.

XLIX   He found her by the ocean's moaning verge,
Nor any wicked change in her discerned;
And she believed his old love had returned,
Which was her exultation, and her scourge.
She took his hand, and walked with him, and seemed
The wife he sought, though shadow-like and dry.
She had one terror, lest her heart should sigh,
And tell her loudly she no longer dreamed.
She dared not say, 'This is my breast: look in.'
But there's a strength to help the desperate weak.
That night he learned how silence best can speak
The awful things when Pity pleads for Sin.
About the middle of the night her call
Was heard, and he came wondering to the bed.
'Now kiss me, dear! it may be, now!' she said.
Lethe had passed those lips, and he knew all.

L   Thus piteously Love closed what he begat:
The union of this ever-diverse pair!
These two were rapid falcons in a snare,
Condemned to do the flitting of the bat.
Lovers beneath the singing sky of May,
They wandered once; clear as the dew on flowers:
But they fed not on the advancing hours:
Their hearts held cravings for the buried day.
Then each applied to each that fatal knife,
Deep questioning, which probes to endless dole.
Ah, what a dusty answer gets the soul
When hot for certainties in this our life!—
In tragic hints here see what evermore
Moves dark as yonder midnight ocean's force,
Thundering like ramping hosts of warrior horse,
To throw that faint thin line upon the shore!

THE OLD CHARTIST

I   Whate'er I be, old England is my dam!
    So there's my answer to the judges, clear.
I'm nothing of a fox, nor of a lamb;
    I don't know how to bleat nor how to leer:
      I'm for the nation!
    That's why you see me by the wayside here,
      Returning home from transportation.

II   It's Summer in her bath this morn, I think.
    I'm fresh as dew, and chirpy as the birds:
And just for joy to see old England wink   10
    Thro' leaves again, I could harangue the herds:
      Isn't it something
    To speak out like a man when you've got words,
      And prove you're not a stupid dumb thing?

III   They shipp'd me off for it; I'm here again.
    Old England is my dam, whate'er I be!
Says I, I'll tramp it home, and see the grain:
    If you see well, you're king of what you see:

Eyesight is having,
If you're not given, I said, to gluttony.   20
Such talk to ignorance sounds as raving.

IV   You dear old brook, that from his Grace's park
           Come bounding! on you run near my old town:
       My lord can't lock the water; nor the lark,
           Unless he kills him, can my lord keep down.
               Up, is the song-note!
           I've tried it, too:—for comfort and renown,
           I rather pitch'd upon the wrong note.

V   I'm not ashamed: Not beaten's still my boast:
           Again I'll rouse the people up to strike.   30
       But home's where different politics jar most.
           Respectability the women like.
               This form, or that form,—
           The Government may be hungry pike,
               But don't you mount a Chartist platform!

VI   Well, well! Not beaten—spite of them, I shout;
           And my estate is suffering for the Cause.—
       Now, what is yon brown water-rat about,
           Who washes his old poll with busy paws?
               What does he mean by 't?   40
           It's like defying all our natural laws,
               For him to hope that he'll get clean by 't.

VII   His seat is on a mud-bank, and his trade
           Is dirt:—he's quite contemptible; and yet
       The fellow's all as anxious as a maid
           To show a decent dress, and dry the wet.
               Now it's his whisker,
           And now his nose, and ear: he seems to get
               Each moment at the motion brisker!

VIII   To see him squat like little chaps at school,   50
           I could let fly a laugh with all my might.
       He peers, hangs both his fore-paws:—bless that fool,
           He's bobbing at his frill now!—what a sight!

Licking the dish up,
As if he thought to pass from black to white,
Like parson into lawny bishop.

IX   The elms and yellow reed-flags in the sun,
           Look on quite grave:—the sunlight flecks his side;
       And links of bindweed-flowers round him run,
           And shine up doubled with him in the tide.   60
               I'm nearly splitting,
           But nature seems like seconding his pride,
           And thinks that his behaviour's fitting.

X   That isle o'mud looks baking dry with gold,
           His needle-muzzle still works out and in.
       It really is a wonder to behold,
           And makes me feel the bristles of my chin.
               Judged by appearance,
           I fancy of the two I'm nearer Sin,
           And might as well commence a clearance.   70

XI   And that's what my fine daughter said:—she meant:
           Pray, hold your tongue, and wear a Sunday face.
       Her husband, the young linendraper, spent
           Much argument thereon:—I'm their disgrace.
               Bother the couple!
           I feel superior to a chap whose place
           Commands him to be neat and supple.

XII   But if I go and say to my old hen:
           I'll mend the gentry's boots, and keep discreet,
       Until they grow *too* violent,—why, then,   80
           A warmer welcome I might chance to meet:
               Warmer and better.
           And if she fancies her old cock is beat,
           And drops upon her knees—so let her!

XIII   She suffered for me:—women, you'll observe,
           Don't suffer for a Cause, but for a man.
       When I was in the dock she show'd her nerve:
           I saw beneath her shawl my old tea-can

53

Trembling . . . she brought it
To screw me for my work: she loath'd my plan,   90
And therefore doubly kind I thought it.

XIV   I've never lost the taste of that same tea:
That liquor on my logic floats like oil,
When I state facts, and fellows disagree.
For human creatures all are in a coil;
All may want pardon.
I see a day when every pot will boil
Harmonious in one great Tea-garden!

XV   We wait the setting of the Dandy's day,
Before that time!—he's furbishing his dress,—   100
He *will* be ready for it!—and I say,
That yon old dandy rat amid the cress,—
Thanks to hard labour!—
If cleanliness is next to godliness,
The old fat fellow's heaven's neighbour!

XVI   You teach me a fine lesson, my old boy!
I've looked on my superiors far too long,
And small has been my profit as my joy.
You've done the right while I've denounced the
wrong.
Prosper me later!   110
Like you I will despise the sniggering throng,
And please myself and my Creator.

XVII   I'll bring the linendraper and his wife
Some day to see you; taking off my hat.
Should they ask why, I'll answer: in my life
I never found so true a democrat.
Base occupation
Can't rob you of your own esteem, old rat!
I'll preach you to the British nation.

I CHAFE AT DARKNESS

I chafe at darkness in the night,
    But when 'tis light,
Hope shuts her eyes; the clouds are pale;
The fields stretch cold into a distance hard:
    I wish again to draw the veil
      Thousand-starred.

Am I of them whose blooms are shed,
    Whose fruits are spent,
Who from dead eyes see Life half-dead;—
Because desire is feeble discontent?   10
    Ah, no! desire and hope should die,
      Thus were I.

But in me something clipped of wing,
    Within its ring
Frets; for I have lost what made
The dawn-breeze magic, and the twilight beam
    A hand with tidings o'er the glade
      Waving seem.

ODE TO THE SPIRIT OF EARTH IN AUTUMN

Fair Mother Earth lay on her back last night,
To gaze her fill on Autumn's sunset skies,
When at a waving of the fallen light,
Sprang realms of rosy fruitage o'er her eyes.
A lustrous heavenly orchard hung the West,
Wherein the blood of Eden bloomed again:
Red were the myriad cherub-mouths that pressed,
Among the clusters, rich with song, full fain,
But dumb, because that overmastering spell
Of rapture held them dumb: then, here and there,   10
A golden harp lost strings; a crimson shell
Burnt grey; and sheaves of lustre fell to air.
The illimitable eagerness of hue
Bronzed, and the beamy winged bloom that flew
'Mid those bunched fruits and thronging figures failed.

A green-edged lake of saffron touched the blue,
With isles of fireless purple lying through:
And Fancy on that lake to seek lost treasures sailed.

     Not long the silence followed:
   The voice that issues from the breast,   20
       O glorious South-west,
   Along the gloom-horizon holloa'd;
Warning the valleys with a mellow roar
Through flapping wings; then sharp the woodland bore
    A shudder and a noise of hands:
    A thousand horns from some far vale
    In ambush sounding on the gale.
    Forth from the cloven sky came bands
Of revel-gathering spirits; trooping down,
Some rode the tree-tops; some on torn cloud-strips,   30
    Burst screaming thro' the lighted town:
And scudding seaward, some fell on big ships:
    Or mounting the sea-horses blew
    Bright foam-flakes on the black review
    Of heaving hulls and burying beaks.

Still on the farthest line, with outpuffed cheeks,
'Twixt dark and utter dark, the great wind drew
From heaven that disenchanted harmony
To join earth's laughter in the midnight blind:
Booming a distant chorus to the shrieks   40
                       Preluding him: then he,
His mantle streaming thunderingly behind,
Across the yellow realm of stiffened Day,
Shot thro' the woodland alleys signals three;
    And with the pressure of a sea,
Plunged broad upon the vale that under lay.

    Night on the rolling foliage fell:
    But I, who love old hymning night,
    And know the Dryad voices well,
    Discerned them as their leaves took flight,   50
    Like souls to wander after death:
    Great armies in imperial dyes,
    And mad to tread the air and rise,

The savage freedom of the skies
To taste before they rot. And here,
Like frail white-bodied girls in fear,
The birches swung from shrieks to sighs;
The aspens, laughers at a breath,
In showering spray-falls mixed their cries,
Or raked a savage ocean-strand   60
With one incessant drowning screech.
Here stood a solitary beech,
That gave its gold with open hand,
And all its branches, toning chill,
Did seem to shut their teeth right fast,
To shriek more mercilessly shrill,
And match the fierceness of the blast.

But heard I a low swell that noised
Of far-off ocean, I was 'ware
Of pines upon their wide roots poised,   70
Whom never madness in the air
Can draw to more than loftier stress
Of mournfulness, not mournfulness
For melancholy, but Joy's excess,
That singing, on the lap of sorrow faints:
And Peace, as in the hearts of saints
Who chant unto the Lord their God;
Deep Peace below upon the muffled sod,
The stillness of the sea's unswaying floor.
Could I be sole there not to see   80
The life within the life awake;
The spirit bursting from the tree,
And rising from the troubled lake?
Pour, let the wines of Heavn pour!
The Golden Harp is struck once more,
And all its music is for me!
Pour, let the wines of Heaven pour!
And, ho, for a night of Pagan glee!

     There is a curtain o'er us.
For once, good souls, we'll not pretend   90
To be aught better than she who bore us,
And is our only visible friend.

Hark to her laughter! who laughs like this,
Can she be dead, or rooted in pain?
She has been slain by the narrow brain,
But for us who love her she lives again.
    Can she die? O, take her kiss!

The crimson-footed nymph is panting up the glade,
With the wine-jar at her arm-pit, and the drunken
    ivy-braid
Round her forehead, breasts, and thighs: starts a
    Satyr, and they speed: 100
Hear the crushing of the leaves: hear the cracking of
    the bough!
And the whistling of the bramble, the piping of the
    weed!

But the bull-voiced oak is battling now:
The storm has seized him half-asleep,
And round him the wild woodland throngs
To hear the fury of his songs,
The uproar of an outraged deep.
He wakes to find a wrestling giant
Trunk to trunk and limb to limb,
And on his rooted force reliant,   110
He laughs and grasps the broadened giant,
And twist and roll the Anakim;
And multitudes acclaiming to the cloud,
    Cry which is breaking, which is bowed.

Away, for the cymbals clash aloft
In the circles of pine, on the moss-floor soft.
The nymphs of the woodland are gathering there.
They huddle the leaves, and trample, and toss;
They swing in the branches, they roll in the moss,
    They blow the seed on the air.   120
Back to back they stand and blow
The winged seed on the cradling air,
A fountain of leaves over bosom and back.
The pipe of the Faun comes on their track,
And the weltering alleys overflow
With musical shrieks and wind-wedded hair.

The riotous companies melt to a pair.
　　Bless them, mother of kindness!

　　A star has nodded through
　　The depths of the flying blue.　　　　　　130
　　Time only to plant the light
　　Of a memory in the blindness.
　　But time to show me the sight
　　Of my life thro' the curtain of night;
　　Shining a moment, and mixed
　　With the onward-hurrying stream,
　　Whose pressure is darkness to me;
　　Behind the curtain, fixed,
　　Beams with endless beam
　　That star on the changing sea.　　　　　　140

Great Mother Nature! teach me, like thee,
To kiss the season and shun regrets.
And am I more than the mother who bore,
Mock me not with thy harmony!
　　Teach me to blot regrets,
　　Great Mother! me inspire
　　With faith that forward sets
　　But feeds the living fire.
　　Faith that never frets
　　For vagueness in the form.　　　　　　150
　　In life, O keep me warm!
　　For, what is human grief?
　　And what do men desire?
Teach me to feel myself the tree,
　　And not the withered leaf.
Fixed am I and await the dark to-be!

　　And O, green bounteous Earth!
Bacchante Mother! stern to those
Who live not in thy heart of mirth;
Death shall I shrink from, loving thee?　　160
Into the breast that gives the rose,
　　Shall I with shuddering fall?

Earth, the mother of all,
Moves on her stedfast way,
Gathering, flinging, sowing.
Mortals, we live in her day,
She in her children is growing.

She can lead us, only she,
Unto God's footstool, whither she reaches:
Loved, enjoyed, her gifts must be,   170
Reverenced the truths she teaches,
Ere a man may hope that he
Ever can attain the glee
Of things without a destiny!

    She knows not loss:
    She feels but her need,
    Who the winged seed
    With the leaf doth toss.

And may not men to this attain?
That the joy of motion, the rapture of being,   180
Shall throw the strong light when our season is fleeing,
Nor quicken aged blood in vain,
At the gates of the vault, on the verge of the plain?
Life thoroughly lived is a fact in the brain,
    While eyes are left for seeing.

Behold, in yon stripped Autumn, shivering grey,
    Earth knows no desolation.
    She smells regeneration
    In the moist breath of decay.

Prophetic of the coming joy and strife,   190
    Like the wild western war-chief sinking
    Calm to the end he eyes unblinking,
Her voice is jubilant in ebbing life.

    He for his happy hunting-fields,
    Forgets the droning chant, and yields
    His numbered breaths to exultation
    In the proud anticipation:

Shouting the glories of his nation,
Shouting the grandeur of his race,
Shouting his own great deeds of daring: 200
And when at last death grasps his face,
And stiffened on the ground in peace
He lies with all his painted terrors glaring;
Hushed are the tribe to hear a threading cry:
      Not from the dead man;
      Not from the standers-by:
      The spirit of the red man
Is welcomed by his fathers up on high.

from **POEMS AND LYRICS OF THE JOY OF EARTH**
   (1883)

A BALLAD OF PAST MERIDIAN

I   Last night returning from my twilight walk
     I met the grey mist Death, whose eyeless brow
     Was bent on me, and from his hand of chalk
     He reached me flowers as from a withered bough:
     O Death, what bitter nosegays givest thou!

II   Death said, I gather, and pursued his way.
     Another stood by me, a shape in stone,
     Sword-hacked and iron-stained, with breasts of clay,
     And metal veins that sometimes fiery shone:
     O Life, how naked and how hard when known!   10

III Life said, As thou hast carved me, such am I.
     Then memory, like the nightjar on the pine,
     And sightless hope, a woodlark in night sky,
     Joined notes of Death and Life till night's decline:
     Of Death, of Life, those inwound notes are mine.

He rises and begins to round,
He drops the silver chain of sound,
Of many links without a break,
In chirrup, whistle, slur and shake,
All intervolved and spreading wide,
Like water-dimples down a tide
Where ripple ripple overcurls
And eddy into eddy whirls;
A press of hurried notes that run
So fleet they scarce are more than one,   10
Yet changeingly the trills repeat
And linger ringing while they fleet,
Sweet to the quick o' the ear, and dear
To her beyond the handmaid ear,
Who sits beside our inner springs,
Too often dry for this he brings,
Which seems the very jet of earth
At sight of sun, her music's mirth,
As up he wings the spiral stair,
A song of light, and pierces air   20
With fountain ardour, fountain play,
To reach the shining tops of day,
And drink in everything discerned
An ecstasy to music turned,
Impelled by what his happy bill
Disperses; drinking, showering still,
Unthinking save that he may give
His voice the outlet, there to live
Renewed in endless notes of glee,
So thirsty of his voice is he,   30
For all to hear and all to know
That he is joy, awake, aglow,
The tumult of the heart to hear
Through pureness filtered crystal-clear,
And know the pleasure sprinkled bright
By simple singing of delight,
Shrill, irreflective, unrestrained,
Rapt, ringing, on the jet sustained
Without a break, without a fall,

Sweet-silvery, sheer lyrical,   40
Perennial, quavering up the chord
Like myriad dews of sunny sward
That trembling into fulness shine,
And sparkle dropping argentine;
Such wooing as the ear receives
From zephyr caught in choric leaves
Of aspens when their chattering net
Is flushed to white with shivers wet;
And such the water-spirit's chime
On mountain heights in morning's prime,   50
Too freshly sweet to seem excess,
Too animate to need a stress;
But wider over many heads
The starry voice ascending spreads,
Awakening, as it waxes thin,
The best in us to him akin;
And every face to watch him raised,
Puts on the light of children praised,
So rich our human pleasure ripes
When sweetness on sincereness pipes,   60
Though nought be promised from the seas,
But only a soft-ruffling breeze
Sweep glittering on a still content,
Serenity in ravishment.

For singing till his heaven fills,
'Tis love of earth that he instils,
And ever winging up and up,
Our valley is his golden cup,
And he the wine which overflows
To lift us with him as he goes: 70
The woods and brooks, the sheep and kine,
He is, the hills, the human line,
The meadows green, the fallows brown,
The dreams of labour in the town;
He sings the sap, the quickened veins;
The wedding song of sun and rains
He is, the dance of children, thanks
Of sowers, shouts of primrose-banks,
And eye of violets while they breathe;

All these the circling song will wreath,   80
And you shall hear the herb and tree,
The better heart of men shall see,
Shall feel celestially, as long
As you crave nothing save the song.

Was never voice of ours could say
Our inmost in the sweetest way,
Like yonder voice aloft, and link
All hearers in the song they drink.
Our wisdom speaks from failing blood,
Our passion is too full in flood,   90
We want the key of his wild note
Of truthful in a tuneful throat,
The song seraphically free
Of taint of personality,
So pure that it salutes the suns
The voice of one for millions,
In whom the millions rejoice
For giving their one spirit voice.

Yet men have we, whom we revere,
Now names, and men still housing here,   100
Whose lives, by many a battle-dint
Defaced, and grinding wheels on flint,
Yield substance, though they sing not, sweet
For song our highest heaven to greet:
Whom heavenly singing gives us new,
Enspheres them brilliant in our blue,
From firmest base to farthest leap,
Because their love of Earth is deep,
And they are warriors in accord
With life to serve, and pass reward,   110
So touching purest and so heard
In the brain's reflex of yon bird:
Wherefore their soul in me, or mine,
Through self-forgetfulness divine,
In them, that song aloft maintains,
To fill the sky and thrill the plains
With showerings drawn from human stores,
As he to silence nearer soars,

Extends the world at wings and dome,
More spacious making more our home,   120
Till lost on his aërial rings
In light, and then the fancy sings.

LOVE IN THE VALLEY

Under yonder beech-tree single on the green-sward,
    Couched with her arms behind her golden head,
Knees and tresses folded to slip and ripple idly,
    Lies my young love sleeping in the shade.
Had I the heart to slide an arm beneath her,
    Press her parting lips as her waist I gather slow,
Waking in amazement she could not but embrace me:
    Then would she hold me and never let me go?

Shy as the squirrel and wayward as the swallow,
    Swift as the swallow along the river's light   10
Circleting the surface to meet his mirrored winglets,
    Fleeter she seems in her stay than in her flight.
Shy as the squirrel that leaps among the pine-tops,
    Wayward as the swallow overhead at set of sun,
She whom I love is hard to catch and conquer,
    Hard, but O the glory of the winning were she won!

When her mother tends her before the laughing mirror,
    Tying up her laces, looping up her hair,
Often she thinks, were this wild thing wedded,
    More love should I have, and much less care.   20
When her mother tends her before the lighted mirror,
    Loosening her laces, combing down her curls,
Often she thinks, were this wild thing wedded,
    I should miss but one for many boys and girls.

Heartless she is as the shadow in the meadows
    Flying to the hills on a blue and breezy noon.
No, she is athirst and drinking up her wonder:
    Earth to her is young as the slip of the new moon.
Deals she an unkindness, 'tis but her rapid measure,
    Even as in a dance; and her smile can heal no less: 30

Like the swinging May-cloud that pelts the flowers with
      hailstones
    Off a sunny border, she was made to bruise and bless.

Lovely are the curves of the white owl sweeping
    Wavy in the dusk lit by one large star.
Lone on the fir-branch, his rattle-note unvaried,
    Brooding o'er the gloom, spins the brown evejar.
Darker grows the valley, more and more forgetting:
    So were it with me if forgetting could be willed.
Tell the grassy hollow that holds the bubbling wellspring;
    Tell it to forget the source that keeps it filled.   40

Stepping down the hill with her fair companions,
    Arm in arm, all against the raying West,
Boldly she sings, to the merry tune she marches,
    Brave is her shape, and sweeter unpossessed.
Sweeter, for she is what my heart first awaking
    Whispered the world was; morning light is she.
Love that so desires would fain keep her changeless;
    Fain would fling the net, and fain have her free.

Happy happy time, when the white star hovers
    Low over dim fields fresh with bloomy dew,   50
Near the face of dawn, that draws athwart the darkness,
    Threading it with colour, as yewberries the yew.
Thicker crowd the shades as the grave East deepens
    Glowing, and with crimson a long cloud swells.
Maiden still the morn is; and strange she is, and secret;
    Strange her eyes; her cheeks are cold as cold seashells.

Sunrays, leaning on our southern hills and lighting
    Wild cloud-mountains that drag the hills along,
Oft ends the day of your shifting brilliant laughter
    Chill as a dull face frowning on a song.   60
Ay, but shows the South-West a ripple-feathered bosom
    Blown to silver while the clouds are shaken and
      ascend
Scaling the mid-heavens as they stream, there comes a
      sunset
    Rich, deep like love in beauty without end.

When at dawn she sighs, and like an infant to the
            window
        Turns grave eyes craving light, released from dreams,
Beautiful she looks, like a white water-lily
        Bursting out of bud in havens of the streams.
When from bed she rises clothed from neck to ankle
        In her long nightgown sweet as boughs of May,   70
Beautiful she looks, like a tall garden lily
        Pure from the night, and splendid for the day.

Mother of the dews, dark eye-lashed twilight,
        Low-lidded twilight, o'er the valley's brim,
Rounding on thy breast sings the dew-delighted skylark,
        Clear as though the dewdrops had their voice in him.
Hidden where the rose-flush drinks the rayless planet,
        Fountain-full he pours the spraying fountain-
            showers.
Let me hear her laughter, I would have her ever
        Cool as dew in twilight, the lark above the flowers. 80

All the girls are out with their baskets for the primrose;
        Up lanes, woods through, they troop in joyful bands.
My sweet leads: she knows not why, but now she loiters,
        Eyes the bent anemones, and hangs her hands.
Such a look will tell that the violets are peeping,
        Coming the rose: and unaware a cry
Springs in her bosom for odours and for colour,
        Covert and the nightingale; she knows not why.

Kerchiefed head and chin she darts between her tulips,
        Streaming like a willow grey in arrowy rain: 90
Some bend beaten cheek to gravel, and their angel
        She will be; she lifts them, and on she speeds again.
Black the driving raincloud breasts the iron gateway:
        She is forth to cheer a neighbour lacking mirth.
So when sky and grass met rolling dumb for thunder
        Saw I once a white dove, sole light of earth.

Prim little scholars are the flowers of her garden,
        Trained to stand in rows, and asking if they please.
I might love them well but for loving more the wild ones:

O my wild ones! they tell me more than these.   100
You, my wild one, you tell of honied field-rose,
    Violet, blushing eglantine in life; and even as they,
They by the wayside are earnest of your goodness,
    You are of life's, on the banks that line the way.

Peering at her chamber the white crowns the red rose,
    Jasmine winds the porch with stars two and three.
Parted is the window; she sleeps; the starry jasmine
    Breathes a falling breath that carries thoughts of me.
Sweeter unpossessed, have I said of her my sweetest?
    Not while she sleeps: while she sleeps the jasmine
        breathes,   110
Luring her to love; she sleeps; the starry jasmine
    Bears me to her pillow under white rose-wreaths.

Yellow with birdfoot-trefoil are the grass-glades;
    Yellow with cinquefoil of the dew-grey leaf;
Yellow with stonecrop; the moss-mounds are yellow;
    Blue-necked the wheat sways, yellowing to the sheaf.
Green-yellow bursts from the copse the laughing yaffle;
    Sharp as a sickle is the edge of shade and shine:
Earth in her heart laughs looking at the heavens,
    Thinking of the harvest: I look and think of mine. 120

This I may know: her dressing and undressing
    Such a change of light shows as when the skies in
        sport
Shift from cloud to moonlight; or edging over thunder
    Slips a ray of sun; or sweeping into port
White sails furl; or on the ocean borders
    White sails lean along the waves leaping green.
Visions of her shower before me, but from eyesight
    Guarded she would be like the sun were she seen.

Front door and back of the mossed old farmhouse
    Open with the morn, and in a breezy link   130
Freshly sparkles garden to stripe-shadowed orchard,
    Green across a rill where on sand the minnows wink.
Busy in the grass the early sun of summer
    Swarms, and the blackbird's mellow fluting notes

Call my darling up with round and roguish challenge:
    Quaintest, richest carol of all the singing throats!

Cool was the woodside; cool as her white dairy
    Keeping sweet the cream-pan; and there the boys
        from school,
Cricketing below, rushed brown and red with sunshine;
    O the dark translucence of the deep-eyed cool!   140
Spying from the farm, herself she fetched a pitcher
    Full of milk, and tilted for each in turn the beak.
Then a little fellow, mouth up and on tiptoe,
    Said, 'I will kiss you': she laughed and leaned her
        cheek.

Doves of the fir-wood walling high our red roof
    Through the long noon coo, crooning through the
        coo.
Loose droop the leaves, and down the sleepy roadway
    Sometimes pipes a chaffinch; loose droops the blue.
Cows flap a slow tail knee-deep in the river,
    Breathless, given up to sun and gnat and fly.   150
Nowhere is she seen; and if I see her nowhere,
    Lightning may come, straight rains and tiger sky.

O the golden sheaf, the rustling treasure-armful!
    O the nutbrown tresses nodding interlaced!
O the treasure-tresses one another over
    Nodding! O the girdle slack about the waist!
Slain are the poppies that shot their random scarlet
    Quick amid the wheatears: would about the waist,
Gathered, see these brides of Earth one blush of ripeness!
    O the nutbrown tresses nodding interlaced!   160

Large and smoky red the sun's cold disk drops,
    Clipped by naked hills, on violet shaded snow:
Eastward large and still lights up a bower of moonrise,
    Whence at her leisure steps the moon aglow.
Nightlong on black print-branches our beech-tree
    Gazes in this whiteness: nightlong could I.
Here may life on death or death on life be painted.
    Let me clasp her soul to know she cannot die!

Gossips count her faults; they scour a narrow chamber
 Where there is no window, read not heaven or
   her.   170
'When she was a tiny,' one aged woman quavers,
 Plucks at my heart and leads me by the ear.
Faults she had once as she learnt to run and tumbled:
 Faults of feature some see, beauty not complete.
Yet, good gossips, beauty that makes holy
 Earth and air, may have faults from head to feet.

Hither she comes; she comes to me; she lingers,
 Deepen her brown eyebrows, while in new surprise
High rise the lashes in wonder of a stranger;
 Yet am I the light and living of her eyes.   180
Something friends have told her fills her heart to
  brimming,
 Nets her in her blushes, and wounds her, and tames.—
Sure of her haven, O like a dove alighting,
 Arms up, she dropped: our souls were in our names.

Soon will she lie like a white-frost sunrise.
 Yellow oats and brown wheat, barley pale as rye,
Long since your sheaves have yielded to the thresher,
 Felt the girdle loosened, seen the tresses fly.
Soon will she lie like a blood-red sunset.
 Swift with the to-morrow, green-winged Spring! 190
Sing from the South-West, bring her back the truants,
 Nightingale and swallow, song and dipping wing.

Soft new beech-leaves, up to beamy April
 Spreading bough on bough a primrose mountain, you
Lucid in the moon, raise lilies to the skyfields,
 Youngest green transfused in silver shining through:
Fairer than the lily, than the wild white cherry:
 Fair as in image my seraph love appears
Borne to me by dreams when dawn is at my eyelids:
 Fair as in the flesh she swims to me on tears.   200

Could I find a place to be alone with heaven,
 I would speak my heart out: heaven is my need.
Every woodland tree is flushing like the dogwood,

Flashing like the whitebeam, swaying like the reed.
Flushing like the dogwood crimson in October;
    Streaming like the flag-reed South-West blown;
Flashing as in gusts the sudden-lighted whitebeam:
    All seem to know what is for heaven alone.

THE ORCHARD AND THE HEATH

I chanced upon an early walk to spy
A troop of children through an orchard gate:
    The boughs hung low, the grass was high;
    They had but to lift hands or wait
For fruits to fill them; fruits were all their sky.

They shouted, running on from tree to tree,
And played the game the wind plays, on and round.
    'Twas visible invisible glee
    Pursuing; and a fountain's sound
Of laughter spouted, pattering fresh on me.   10

I could have watched them till the daylight fled,
Their pretty bower made such a light of day.
    A small one tumbling sang, 'Oh! head!'
    The rest to comfort her straightway
Seized on a branch and thumped down apples red.

The tiny creature flashing through green grass,
And laughing with her feet and eyes among
    Fresh apples, while a little lass
    Over as o'er breeze-ripples hung:
That sight I saw, and passed as aliens pass.   20

My footpath left the pleasant farms and lanes,
Soft cottage-smoke, straight cocks a-crow, gay flowers;
    Beyond the wheel-ruts of the wains,
    Across a heath I walked for hours,
And met its rival tenants, rays and rains.

Still in my view mile-distant firs appeared,
When, under a patched channel-bank enriched

With foxglove whose late bells drooped seared,
  Behold, a family had pitched
Their camp, and labouring the low tent upreared.   30

Here, too, were many children, quick to scan
A new thing coming; swarthy cheeks, white teeth:
  In many-coloured rags they ran,
  Like iron runlets of the heath.
Dispersed lay broth-pot, sticks, and drinking-can.

Three girls, with shoulders like a boat at sea
Tipped sideways by the wave (their clothing slid
  From either ridge unequally),
  Lean, swift and voluble, bestrid
A starting-point, unfrocked to the bent knee.   40

They raced; their brothers yelled them on, and broke
In act to follow, but as one they snuffed
  Wood-fumes, and by the fire that spoke
  Of provender, its pale flame puffed,
And rolled athwart dwarf furzes grey-blue smoke.

Soon on the dark edge of a ruddier gleam,
The mother-pot perusing, all, stretched flat,
  Paused for its bubbling-up supreme:
  A dog upright in circle sat,
And oft his nose went with the flying steam.   50

I turned and looked on heaven awhile, where now
The moor-faced sunset broaden'd with red light;
  Threw high aloft a golden bough,
  And seemed the desert of the night
Far down with mellow orchards to endow.

LUCIFER IN STARLIGHT

On a starred night Prince Lucifer uprose.
Tired of his dark dominion swung the fiend
Above the rolling ball in cloud part screened,
Where sinners hugged their spectre of repose.

Poor prey to his hot fit of pride were those.
And now upon his western wing he leaned,
Now his huge bulk o'er Afric's sands careened,
Now the black planet shadowed Arctic snows.
Soaring through wider zones that pricked his scars
With memory of the old revolt from Awe,   10
He reached a middle height, and at the stars,
Which are the brain of heaven, he looked, and sank.
Around the ancient track marched, rank on rank,
The army of unalterable law.

A LATER ALEXANDRIAN

An inspiration caught from dubious hues,
Filled him, and mystic wrynesses he chased;
For they lead farther than the single-faced,
Wave subtler promise when desire pursues.
The moon of cloud discoloured was his Muse,
His pipe the reed of the old moaning waste.
Love was to him with anguish fast enlaced,
And Beauty where she walked blood-shot the dews.
Men railed at such a singer; women thrilled
Responsively: he sang not Nature's own   10
Divinest, but his lyric had a tone,
As 'twere a forest-echo of her voice:
What barrenly they yearn for seemed distilled
From what they dread, who do through tears rejoice.

from **BALLADS AND POEMS OF TRAGIC LIFE (1887)**

KING HARALD'S TRANCE

I   Sword in length a reaping-hook amain
Harald sheared his field, blood up to shank:
    'Mid the swathes of slain,
    First at moonrise drank.

II   Thereof hunger, as for meats the knife,
       Pricked his ribs, in one sharp spur to reach
           Home and his young wife,
           Nigh the sea-ford beach.

III   After battle keen to feed was he:
       Smoking flesh the thresher washed down fast,   10
           Like an angry sea
           Ships from keel to mast.

IV   Name us glory, singer, name us pride
       Matching Harald's in his deeds of strength;
           Chiefs, wife, sword by side,
           Foemen stretched their length!

V   Half a winter night the toasts hurrahed,
       Crowned him, clothed him, trumpeted him high,
           Till awink he bade
           Wife to chamber fly.   20

VI   Twice the sun had mounted, twice had sunk,
       Ere his ears took sound; he lay for dead;
           Mountain on his trunk,
           Ocean on his head.

VII   Clamped to couch, his fiery hearing sucked
       Whispers that at heart made iron-clang:
           Here fool-women clucked,
           There men held harangue.

VIII Burial to fit their lord of war,
       They decreed him: hailed the kingling: ha!   30
           Hateful! but this Thor
           Failed a weak lamb's baa.

IX   King they hailed a branchlet, shaped to fare,
       Weighted so, like quaking shingle spume,
           When his blood's own heir
           Ripened in the womb!

X   Still he heard, and doglike, hoglike, ran
       Nose of hearing till his blind sight saw:
          Woman stood with man
          Mouthing low, at paw.   40

XI   Woman, man, they mouthed; they spake a thing
       Armed to split a mountain, sunder seas:
          Still the frozen king
          Lay and felt him freeze.

XII   Doglike, hoglike, horselike now he raced,
       Riderless, in ghost across a ground
          Flint of breast, blank-faced,
          Past the fleshly bound.

XIII   Smell of brine his nostrils filled with might:
       Nostrils quickened eyelids, eyelids hand: 50
          Hand for sword at right
          Groped, the great haft spanned.

XIV   Wonder struck to ice his people's eyes:
       Him they saw, the prone upon the bier,
          Sheer from backbone rise,
          Sword uplifting peer.

XV   Sitting did he breathe against the blade,
       Standing kiss it for that proof of life:
          Strode, as netters wade,
          Straightway to his wife.   60

XVI   Her he eyed: his judgement was one word,
       Foulbed! and she fell: the blow clove two.
          Fearful for the third,
          All their breath indrew.

XVII   Morning danced along the waves to beach;
       Dumb his chiefs fetched breath for what might hap:
          Glassily on each
          Stared the iron cap.

XVIII Sudden, as it were a monster oak
        Split to yield a limb by stress of heat,   70
            Strained he, staggered, broke
            Doubled at their feet.

from **A READING OF EARTH (1888)**

HARD WEATHER

    Bursts from a rending East in flaws
    The young green leaflet's harrier, sworn
    To strew the garden, strip the shaws,
    And show our Spring with banner torn.
    Was ever such virago morn?
    The wind has teeth, the wind has claws,
    All the wind's wolves through woods are loose,
    The wild wind's falconry aloft.
    Shrill underfoot the grassblade shrews,
    At gallop, clumped, and down the croft   10
    Bestrid by shadows, beaten, tossed;
    It seems a scythe, it seems a rod.
    The howl is up at the howl's accost;
    The shivers greet and the shivers nod.

    Is the land ship? we are rolled, we drive
    Tritonly, cleaving hiss and hum;
    Whirl with the dead, or mount or dive,
    Or down in dregs, or on in scum.
    And drums the distant, pipes the near,
    And vale and hill are grey in grey,   20
    As when the surge is crumbling sheer,
    And sea-mews wing the haze of spray.
    Clouds—are they bony witches?—swarms,
    Darting swift on the robber's flight,
    Hurry an infant sky in arms:
    It peeps, it becks; 'tis day, 'tis night.
    Black while over the loop of blue
    The swathe is closed, like shroud on corse.

Lo, as if swift the Furies flew,
The Fates at heel at a cry to horse! 30

Interpret me the savage whirr:
And is it Nature scourged, or she,
Her offspring's executioner,
Reducing land to barren sea?
But is there meaning in a day
When this fierce angel of the air,
Intent to throw, and haply slay,
Can for what breath of life we bear,
Exact the wrestle? Call to mind
The many meanings glistening up 40
When Nature to her nurselings kind,
Hands them the fruitage and the cup!
And seek we rich significance
Not otherwhere than with those tides
Of pleasure on the sunned expanse,
Whose flow deludes, whose ebb derides?

Look in the face of men who fare
Lock-mouthed, a match in lungs and thews
For this fierce angel of the air,
To twist with him and take his bruise. 50
That is the face beloved of old
Of Earth, young mother of her brood:
Nor broken for us shows the mould
When muscle is in mind renewed:
Though farther from her nature rude,
Yet nearer to her spirit's hold:
And though of gentler mood serene,
Still forceful of her fountain-jet.
So shall her blows be shrewdly met,
Be luminously read the scene 60
Where Life is at her grindstone set,
That she may give us edgeing keen,
String us for battle, till as play
The common strokes of fortune shower.
Such meaning in a dagger-day
Our wits may clasp to wax in power.
Yea, feel us warmer at her breast,

By spin of blood in lusty drill,
Than when her honeyed hands caressed,
And Pleasure, sapping, seemed to fill. 70

Behold the life at ease; it drifts.
The sharpened life commands its course.
She winnows, winnows roughly; sifts,
To dip her chosen in her source:
Contention is the vital force,
Whence pluck they brain, her prize of gifts,
Sky of the senses! on which height,
Not disconnected, yet released,
They see how spirit comes to light,
Through conquest of the inner beast, 80
Which Measure tames to movement sane,
In harmony with what is fair.
Never is Earth misread by brain:
That is the welling of her, there
The mirror: with one step beyond,
For likewise is it voice; and more,
Benignest kinship bids respond,
When wail the weak, and them restore
Whom days as fell as this may rive,
While Earth sits ebon in her gloom, 90
Us atomies of life alive
Unheeding, bent on life to come.
Her children of the labouring brain,
These are the champions of the race,
True parents, and the sole humane,
With understanding for their base.
Earth yields the milk, but all her mind
Is vowed to thresh for stouter stock.
Her passion for old giantkind,
That scaled the mount, uphurled the rock, 100
Devolves on them who read aright
Her meaning and devoutly serve;
Nor in her starlessness of night
Peruse her with the craven nerve:
But even as she from grass to corn,
To eagle high from grubbing mole,
Prove in strong brain her noblest born,
The station for the flight of soul.

THE THRUSH IN FEBRUARY

I know him, February's thrush,
And loud at eve he valentines
On sprays that paw the naked bush
Where soon will sprout the thorns and bines.

Now ere the foreign singer thrills
Our vale his plain-song pipe he pours,
A herald of the million bills;
And heed him not, the loss is yours.

My study, flanked with ivied fir
And budded beech with dry leaves curled,   10
Perched over yew and juniper,
He neighbours, piping to his world:—

The wooded pathways dank on brown,
The branches on grey cloud a web,
The long green roller of the down,
An image of the deluge-ebb:—

And farther, they may hear along
The stream beneath the poplar row,
By fits, like welling rocks, the song
Spouts of a blushful Spring in flow.   20

But most he loves to front the vale
When waves of warm South-western rains
Have left our heavens clear in pale,
With faintest beck of moist red veins:

Vermilion wings, by distance held
To pause aflight while fleeting swift:
And high aloft the pearl inshelled
Her lucid glow in glow will lift;

A little south of coloured sky;
Directing, gravely amorous,   30
The human of a tender eye
Through pure celestial on us:

Remote, not alien; still, not cold;
Unraying yet, more pearl than star;
She seems a while the vale to hold
In trance, and homelier makes the far.

Then Earth her sweet unscented breathes;
An orb of lustre quits the height;
And like broad iris-flags, in wreaths
The sky takes darkness, long ere quite.   40

His Island voice then shall you hear,
Nor even after separate
From such a twilight of the year
Advancing to the vernal gate.

He sings me, out of Winter's throat,
The young time with the life ahead;
And my young time his leaping note
Recalls to spirit-mirth from dead.

Imbedded in a land of greed,
Of mammon-quakings dire as Earth's,   50
My care was but to soothe my need;
At peace among the littleworths.

To light and song my yearning aimed;
To that deep breast of song and light
Which men have barrenest proclaimed;
As 'tis to senses pricked with fright.

So mine are these new fruitings rich
The simple to the common brings;
I keep the youth of souls who pitch
Their joy in this old heart of things: 60

Who feel the Coming young as aye,
Thrice hopeful on the ground we plough;
Alive for life, awake to die;
One voice to cheer the seedling Now.

Full lasting is the song, though he,
The singer, passes: lasting too,
For souls not lent in usury,
The rapture of the forward view.

With that I bear my senses fraught
Till what I am fast shoreward drives.   70
They are the vessel of the Thought.
The vessel splits, the Thought survives.

Nought else are we when sailing brave,
Save husks to raise and bid it burn.
Glimpse of its livingness will wave
A light the senses can discern

Across the river of the death,
Their close. Meanwhile, O twilight bird
Of promise! bird of happy breath!
I hear, I would the City heard.   80

The City of the smoky fray;
A prodded ox, it drags and moans:
Its Morrow no man's child; its Day
A vulture's morsel beaked to bones.

It strives without a mark for strife;
It feasts beside a famished host:
The loose restraint of wanton life,
That threatened penance in the ghost!

Yet there our battle urges; there
Spring heroes many; issuing thence,   90
Names that should leave no vacant air
For fresh delight in confidence.

Life was to them the bag of grain,
And Death the weedy harrow's tooth.
Those warriors of the sighting brain
Give worn Humanity new youth.

Our song and star are they to lead
The tidal multitude and blind
From bestial to the higher breed
By fighting souls of love divined.   100

They scorned the ventral dream of peace,
Unknown in nature. This they knew:
That life begets with fair increase
Beyond the flesh, if life be true.

Just reason based on valiant blood,
The instinct bred afield would match
To pipe thereof a swelling flood,
Were men of Earth made wise in watch.

Though now the numbers count as drops
An urn might bear, they father Time.   110
She shapes anew her dusty crops;
Her quick in their own likeness climb.

Of their own force do they create;
They climb to light, in her their root.
Your brutish cry at muffled fate
She smites with pangs of worse than brute.

She, judged of shrinking nerves, appears
A Mother whom no cry can melt;
But read her past desires and fears,
The letters on her breast are spelt.   120

A slayer, yea, as when she pressed
Her savage to the slaughter-heaps,
To sacrifice she prompts her best:
She reaps them as the sower reaps.

But read her thought to speed the race,
And stars rush forth of blackest night:
You chill not at a cold embrace
To come, nor dread a dubious might.

Her double visage, double voice,
In oneness rise to quench the doubt.   130
This breath, her gift, has only choice
Of service, breathe we in or out.

Since Pain and Pleasure on each hand
Led our wild steps from slimy rock
To yonder sweeps of gardenland,
We breathe but to be sword or block.

The sighting brain her good decree
Accepts; obeys those guides, in faith,
By reason hourly fed, that she,
To some the clod, to some the wraith,   140

Is more, no mask; a flame, a stream.
Flame, stream, are we, in mid career
From torrent source, delirious dream,
To heaven-reflecting currents clear.

And why the sons of Strength have been
Her cherished offspring ever; how
The Spirit served by her is seen
Through Law; perusing love will show.

Love born of knowledge, love that gains
Vitality as Earth it mates,   150
The meaning of the Pleasures, Pains,
The Life, the Death, illuminates.

For love we Earth, then serve we all;
Her mystic secret then is ours:
We fall, or view our treasures fall,
Unclouded, as beholds her flowers

Earth, from a night of frosty wreck,
Enrobed in morning's mounted fire,
When lowly, with a broken neck,
The crocus lays her cheek to mire.   160

OUTER AND INNER

I   From twig to twig the spider weaves
        At noon his webbing fine.
    So near to mute the zephyrs flute
        That only leaflets dance.
    The sun draws out of hazel leaves
        A smell of woodland wine.
    I wake a swarm to sudden storm
        At any step's advance.

II   Along my path is bugloss blue,
        The star with fruit in moss;   10
    The foxgloves drop from throat to top
        A daily lesser bell.
    The blackest shadow, nurse of dew,
        Has orange skeins across;
    And keenly red is one thin thread
        That flashing seems to swell.

III   My world I note ere fancy comes,
        Minutest hushed observe:
    What busy bits of motioned wits
        Through antlered mosswork strive.   20
    But now so low the stillness hums,
        My springs of seeing swerve,
    For half a wink to thrill and think
        The woods with nymphs alive.

IV   I neighbour the invisible
        So close that my consent
    Is only asked for spirits masked
        To leap from trees and flowers.
    And this because with them I dwell
        In thought, while calmly bent   30
    To read the lines dear Earth designs
        Shall speak her life on ours.

V   Accept, she says; it is not hard
        In woods; but she in towns
    Repeats, accept; and have we wept,

And have we quailed with fears,
Or shrunk with horrors, sure reward
   We have whom knowledge crowns;
Who see in mould the rose unfold,
   The soul through blood and tears.

DIRGE IN WOODS

A wind sways the pines,
   And below
Not a breath of wild air;
Still as the mosses that glow
On the flooring and over the lines
Of the roots here and there.
The pine-tree drops its dead;
They are quiet, as under the sea.
Overhead, overhead
Rushes life in a race,   10
As the clouds the clouds chase;
   And we go,
And we drop like the fruits of the tree,
   Even we,
   Even so.

CHANGE IN RECURRENCE

I   I stood at the gate of the cot
Where my darling, with side-glance demure,
Would spy, on her trim garden-plot,
The busy wild things chase and lure.
For these with their ways were her feast
They had surety no enemy lurked.
Their deftest of tricks to their least,
She gathered in watch as she worked.

II   When berries were red on her ash,
The blackbird would rifle them rough,   10
Till the ground underneath looked a gash,
And her rogue grew the round of a chough.

The squirrel cocked ear o'er his hoop,
Up the spruce, quick as eye, trailing brush.
She knew any tit of the troop
All as well as the snail-tapping thrush.

III   I gazed: 'twas the scene of the frame,
With the face, the dear life for me, fled.
No window a lute to my name,
No watcher there plying the thread.   20
But the blackbird hung pecking at will;
The squirrel from cone hopped to cone;
The thrush had a snail in his bill,
And tap-tapped the shell hard on a stone.

HYMN TO COLOUR

I   With Life and Death I walked when Love appeared,
And made them on each side a shadow seem.
Through wooded vales the land of dawn we neared,
Where down smooth rapids whirls the helmless dream
To fall on daylight; and night puts away
      Her darker veil for grey.

II   In that grey veil green grassblades brushed we by;
We came where woods breathed sharp, and overhead
Rocks raised clear horns on a transforming sky:
Around, save for those shapes, with him who led   10
And linked them, desert varied by no sign
      Of other life than mine.

III   By this the dark-winged planet, raying wide,
From the mild pearl-glow to the rose upborne,
Drew in his fires, less faint than far descried,
Pure-fronted on a stronger wave of morn:
And those two shapes the splendour interweaved
      Hung web-like, sank and heaved.

IV   Love took my hand when hidden stood the sun
To fling his robe on shoulder-heights of snow.   20
Then said: There lie they, Life and Death in one.

Whichever is, the other is: but know,
It is thy craving self that thou dost see,
    Not in them seeing me.

V   Shall man into the mystery of breath,
From his quick beating pulse a pathway spy?
Or learn the secret of the shrouded death,
By lifting up the lid of a white eye?
Cleave thou thy way with fathering desire
    Of fire to reach to fire.   30

VI   Look now where Colour, the soul's bridegroom, makes
The house of heaven splendid for the bride.
To him as leaps a fountain she awakes,
In knotting arms, yet boundless: him beside,
She holds the flower to heaven, and by his power
    Brings heaven to the flower.

VII   He gives her homeliness in desert air,
And sovereignty in spaciousness; he leads
Through widening chambers of surprise to where
Throbs rapture near an end that aye recedes,   40
Because his touch is infinite and lends
    A yonder to all ends.

VIII Death begs of Life his blush; Life Death persuades
To keep long day with his caresses graced.
He is the heart of light, the wing of shades,
The crown of beauty: never soul embraced
Of him can harbour unfaith; soul of him
    Possessed walks never dim.

IX   Love eyed his rosy memories: he sang:
O bloom of dawn, breathed up from the gold sheaf   50
Held springing beneath Orient! that dost hang
The space of dewdrops running over leaf;
Thy fleetingness is bigger in the ghost
    Than Time with all his host!

X   Of thee to say behold, has said adieu:
But love remembers how the sky was green,

And how the grasses glimmered lightest blue;
How saint-like grey took fervour: how the screen
Of cloud grew violet; how thy moment came
      Between a blush and flame.   60

XI   Love saw the emissary eglantine
Break wave round thy white feet above the gloom;
Lay finger on thy star; thy raiment line
With cherub wing and limb; wed thy soft bloom,
Gold-quivering like sunrays in thistle-down,
      Earth under rolling brown.

XII   They do not look through love to look on thee,
Grave heavenliness! nor know they joy of sight,
Who deem the wave of rapt desire must be
Its wrecking and last issue of delight.   70
Dead seasons quicken in one petal-spot
      Of colour unforgot.

XIII This way have men come out of brutishness
To spell the letters of the sky and read
A reflex upon earth else meaningless.
With thee, O fount of the Untimed! to lead;
Drink they of thee, thee eyeing, they unaged
      Shall on through brave wars waged.

XIV More gardens will they win than any lost;
The vile plucked out of them, the unlovely slain.   80
Not forfeiting the beast with which they are crossed,
To stature of the Gods will they attain.
They shall uplift their Earth to meet her Lord,
      Themselves the attuning chord!

XV   The song had ceased; my vision with the song.
Then of those Shadows, which one made descent
Beside me I knew not: but Life ere long
Came on me in the public ways and bent
Eyes deeper than of old: Death met I too,
      And saw the dawn glow through.   90

from **MODERN LOVE, A REPRINT** (1892)

THE LESSON OF GRIEF

> Not ere the bitter herb we taste,
> Which ages thought of happy times,
> To plant us in a weeping waste,
> Rings with our fellows this one heart
>   Accordant chimes.
>
> When I had shed my glad year's leaf,
> I did believe I stood alone,
> Till that great company of Grief
> Taught me to know this craving heart
>   For not my own.   10

from **POEMS: THE EMPTY PURSE** (1892)

NIGHT OF FROST IN MAY

> With splendour of a silver day,
> A frosted night had opened May:
> And on that plumed and armoured night,
> As one close temple hove our wood,
> Its border leafage virgin white.
> Remote down air an owl hallooed.
> The black twig dropped without a twirl;
> The bud in jewelled grasp was nipped;
> The brown leaf cracked a scorching curl;
> A crystal off the green leaf slipped.   10
> Across the tracks of rimy tan,
> Some busy thread at whiles would shoot;
> A limping minnow-rillet ran,
> To hang upon an icy foot.
>
> In this shrill hush of quietude,
> The ear conceived a severing cry.
> Almost it let the sound elude,
> When chuckles three, a warble shy,
> From hazels of the garden came,

Near by the crimson-windowed farm. 20
They laid the trance on breath and frame,
A prelude of the passion-charm.

Then soon was heard, not sooner heard
Than answered, doubled, trebled, more,
Voice of an Eden in the bird
Renewing with his pipe of four
The sob: a troubled Eden, rich
In throb of heart: unnumbered throats
Flung upward at a fountain's pitch,
The fervour of the four long notes, 30
That on the fountain's pool subside,
Exult and ruffle and upspring:
Endless the crossing multiplied
Of silver and of golden string.
There chimed a bubbled underbrew
With witch-wild spray of vocal dew.

It seemed a single harper swept
Our wild wood's inner chords and waked
A spirit that for yearning ached
Ere men desired and joyed or wept. 40
Or now a legion ravishing
Musician rivals did unite
In love of sweetness high to sing
The subtle song that rivals light;
From breast of earth to breast of sky:
And they were secret, they were nigh:
A hand the magic might disperse;
The magic swung my universe.

Yet sharpened breath forbade to dream,
Where all was visionary gleam; 50
Where Seasons, as with cymbals, clashed;
And feelings, passing joy and woe,
Churned, gurgled, spouted, interflashed,
Nor either was the one we know:
Nor pregnant of the heart contained
In us were they, that griefless plained,
That plaining soared; and through the heart

Struck to one note the wide apart:—
A passion surgent from despair;
A paining bliss in fervid cold;   60
Off the last vital edge of air,
Leap heavenward of the lofty-souled,
For rapture of a wine of tears;
As had a star among the spheres
Caught up our earth to some mid-height
Of double life to ear and sight,
She giving voice to thought that shines
Keen-brilliant of her deepest mines;
While steely drips the rillet clinked,
And hoar with crust the cowslip swelled.   70

Then was the lyre of earth beheld,
Then heard by me: it holds me linked;
Across the years to dead-ebb shores
I stand on, my blood-thrill restores.
But would I conjure into me
Those issue notes, I must review
What serious breath the woodland drew;
The low throb of expectancy;
How the white mother-muteness pressed
On leaf and meadow-herb; how shook,   80
Nigh speech of mouth, the sparkle-crest
Seen spinning on the bracken-crook.

from **A READING OF LIFE** (1901)

SONG IN THE SONGLESS

They have no song, the sedges dry,
    And still they sing.
It is within my breast they sing,
    As I pass by.
Within my breast they touch a string,
    They wake a sigh.
There is but sound of sedges dry;
    In me they sing.

IN THE WOODS

I   Hill-sides are dark,
And hill-tops reach the star,
       And down is the lark,
       And I from my mark
         Am far.

Unlighted I foot the ways.
I know that a dawn is before me,
And behind me many days;
      Not what is o'er me.

II   I am in deep woods,   10
      Between the two twilights.

Whatsoever I am and may be,
Write it down to the light in me;
I am I, and it is my deed;
For I know that paths are dark
      Between the two twilights:

My foot on the nodding weed,
My hand on the wrinkled bark,
I have made my choice to proceed
By the light I have within;   20
And the issue rests with me,
Who might sleep in a chrysalis,
In the fold of a simple prayer,
      Between the two twilights:

Flying safe from even to morn:
Not stumbling abroad in air
That shudders to touch and to kiss,
And is unfraternal and thin:
Self-hunted in it, forlorn,
Unloved, unresting, bare,   30
      Between the two twilights:

Having nought but the light in me,
Which I take for my soul in arms,
Resolved to go unto the wells
For water, rejecting spells,
And mouthings of magic for charms,
And the cup that does not flow.

    I am in deep woods
        Between the two twilights:

Over valley and hill   40
I hear the woodland wave,
Like the voice of Time, as slow,
The voice of Life, as grave,
The voice of Death, as still.

III   Take up thy song from woods and fields
Whilst thou hast heart, and living yields
        Delight: let that expire—
Let thy delight in living die,
Take thou thy song from star and sky,
        And join the silent quire.   50

IV   With the butterfly roaming abroad
        On the sunny March day,
The pine-cones opened and blew
Winged seeds, and aloft they flew
Butterfly-like in the ray,
        And hung to the breeze:
Spinning they fell to the sod.
        Ask you my rhyme
        Which shall be trees?
        They have had their time.   60

V   I know that since the hour of birth,
        Rooted in earth,
        I have looked above,
        In joy and in grief,
        With eyes of belief,
           For love.
        A mother trains us so.

But the love I saw was a fitful thing;
        I looked on the sun
        That clouds or is blinding aglow: 70
    And the love around had more of wing
    Than substance, and of spirit none.

Then looked I on the green earth we are rooted in,
        Whereof we grow,
        And nothing of love it said,
        But gave me warnings of sin,
        And lessons of patience let fall,
        And told how pain was bred,
        And wherefore I was weak,
        And of good and evil at strife,   80
        And the struggle upward of all,
    And my choice of the glory of life:
            Was love farther to seek?

VI   The lover of life holds life in his hand,
        Like a ring for the bride.
    The lover of life is free of dread:
    The lover of life holds life in his hand,
        As the hills hold the day.

But lust after life waves life like a brand,
        For an ensign of pride.   90
    The lust after life is life half-dead:
    Yea, lust after life hugs life like a brand,
        Dreading air and the ray.

            For the sake of life,
            For that life is dear,
            The lust after life
            Clings to it fast.
            For the sake of life,
            For that life is fair,
            The lover of life   100
            Flings it broadcast.

The lover of life knows his labour divine,
    And therein is at peace.

The lust after life craves a touch and a sign
  That the life shall increase.

The lust after life in the chills of its lust
  Claims a passport of death.
The lover of life sees the flame in our dust
  And a gift in our breath.

THE FAIR BEDFELLOW

I remember, long ago,
  Ere my teens were twelve & one,
With a fair bedfellow
  I was warm till morning's sun.

Years she had that doubled mine:
  And I puzzled to divine
When at night I started
Why I always found her crying
  She was crying broken-hearted.

By a lamp on the bed,   10
  Lifting slightly on her knees,
Trembling letter-sheets she read,
  Clasping beads from foreign seas.

With her forehead on them bow'd
  Broken words, & half-aloud,
Read she—all her body shaking—
Till my heart nigh burst with aching.

Then her neck I took with a leap
  In my arms, & sought to know
What it was that made her weep,   20
  My own darling bedfellow.

And she kissed me, made the room
Soft again with tender gloom:
In against her bosom drew me
Till her dear heart panted thro' me.

AIMÉE

On that great night of her success,
When by her mirror she disrobed;
A finger's dubitative press
She laid on her pulse, as one who probed,
Yet found no shot, nor sounded the deep void;
And sternly at the reflex of her frown
She gazed unthinking, save that unenjoyed
Was now the ripe fruit showering down,
Once coveted, too long witheld;
Sharp with the pain of pleasure dead.   10

APPENDIX

LOVE IN THE VALLEY
(First version, from *POEMS*, 1851)

Under yonder beech-tree standing on the green-sward,
   Couched with her arms behind her little head,
Her knees folded up, and her tresses on her bosom,
   Lies my young love sleeping in the shade.
Had I the heart to slide one arm beneath her,
   Press her dreaming lips as her waist I folded slow,
Waking on the instant she could not but embrace me—
   Ah! would she hold me, and never let me go?

Shy as the squirrel, and wayward as the swallow;
   Swift as the swallow when athwart the western
      flood   10
Circleting the surface he meets his mirrored winglets,—
   Is that dear one in her maiden bud.
Shy as the squirrel whose nest is in the pine-tops;
   Gentle—ah! that she were jealous as the dove!
Full of all the wildness of the woodland creatures,
   Happy in herself is the maiden that I love!

What can have taught her distrust of all I tell her?
   Can she truly doubt me when looking on my brows?
Nature never teaches distrust of tender love-tales,

What can have taught her distrust of all my vows?   20
No, she does not doubt me! on a dewy eve-tide
  Whispering together beneath the listening moon,
I pray'd till her cheek flush'd, implored till she faltered—
  Fluttered to my bosom—ah! to fly away so soon!

When her mother tends her before the laughing mirror,
  Tying up her laces, looping up her hair,
Often she thinks—were this wild thing wedded,
  I should have more love, and much less care.
When her mother tends her before the bashful mirror,
  Loosening her laces, combing down her curls,   30
Often she thinks—were this wild thing wedded,
  I should lose but one for so many boys and girls.

Clambering roses peep into her chamber,
  Jasmine and woodbine breathe sweet, sweet,
White-necked swallows twittering of summer,
  Fill her with balm and nested peace from head to feet.
Ah! will the rose-bough see her lying lonely,
  When the petals fall and fierce bloom is on the leaves?
Will the Autumn garners see her still ungathered,
  When the fickle swallows forsake the weeping
    eaves?   40

Comes a sudden question—should a strange hand pluck
    her!
  Oh! what an anguish smites me at the thought.
Should some idle lordling bribe her mind with jewels!—
  Can such beauty ever thus be bought?
Sometimes the huntsmen prancing down the valley
  Eye the village lasses, full of sprightly mirth;
They see as I see, mine is the fairest!
  Would she were older and could read my worth!

Are there not sweet maidens if she still deny me?
  Show the bridal heavens but one bright star?   50
Wherefore thus then do I chase a shadow,
  Clattering one note like a brown eve-jar?
So I rhyme and reason till she darts before me—
  Thro' the milky meadows from flower to flower she
    flies,

Sunning her sweet palms to shade her dazzled eyelids
   From the golden love that looks too eager in her
      eyes.

When at dawn she wakens, and her fair face gazes
   Out on the weather thro' the window-panes,
Beauteous she looks! like a white water-lily
   Bursting out of bud on the rippled river plains.   60
When from bed she rises clothed from neck to ankle
   In her long nightgown, sweet as boughs of May,
Beauteous she looks! like a tall garden lily
   Pure from the night and perfect for the day!

Happy, happy time, when the grey star twinkles
   Over the fields all fresh with bloomy dew;
When the cold-cheeked dawn grows ruddy up the
      twilight,
   And the gold sun wakes, and weds her in the blue.
Then when my darling tempts the early breezes,
   She the only star that dies not with the dark!   70
Powerless to speak all the ardour of my passion
   I catch her little hand as we listen to the lark.

Shall the birds in vain then valentine their sweethearts?
   Season after season tell a fruitless tale;
Will not the virgin listen to their voices?
   Take the honeyed meaning, wear the bridal veil.
Fears she frosts of winter, fears she the bare branches?
   Waits she the garlands of spring for her dower?
Is she a nightingale that will not be nested
   Till the April woodland has built her bridal
      bower?   80

Then come merry April with all thy birds and beauties!
   With thy crescent brows and thy flowery, showery
      glee;
With thy budding leafage and fresh green pastures;
   And may thy lustrous crescent grow a honeymoon
      for me!

Come merry month of the cuckoo and the violet!
Come weeping Loveliness in all thy blue delight!
Lo! the nest is ready, let me not languish longer!
Bring her to my arms on the first May night.

NOTES

Details of editions and studies of Meredith cited below in an abbreviated form are given in Principal Editions and the Selected Bibliography. The poems in bold print are in this selection.

INTRODUCTION

I LIFE

1   G. K. Chesterton, *The Victorian Age in Literature*, 2nd edition, London, 1966, p.62.
2   'George Meredith', *The Variorum Edition of the Complete Poems of Thomas Hardy*, ed. James Gibson, 1979, p.298, l.6.
3   Lionel Stevenson, *The Ordeal*, p.346.
4   Quoted by John Press, *A Map of Modern English Verse*, Oxford, 1969, p.1.

II THOUGHT

1   *The Poems of Tennyson*, ed. Christopher Ricks, London, 1969, p.910, IV, l.8.
2   Preface to *Lyrical Ballads, The Prose works of William Wordsworth*, ed. W. J. B. Owen and J. W. Smyser, 3 vols., Oxford, 1974, I, 141.
3   'Earth and Man', *The Poems*, ed. Bartlett, I, 266, IV, ll.2-3.
4   *Aspects of the Novel*, Harmondsworth, 1962, p.97.
5   **The Lesson of Grief**, ll.7-10.
6   'Foresight and Patience', *The Poems*, ed. Bartlett, I, 694, l.264.
7   'Ode to Duty', *The Poetical Works of William Wordsworth*, ed. E. de Selincourt and H. Darbishire, 5 vols., Oxford, 1940-9, IV, l.48.
8   'The Woods of Westermain', *The Poems*, ed. Bartlett, I, 210, III, ll.94-6.
9   **The Thrush in February**, ll.103-4.
10   'The Test of Manhood', *The Poems*, ed. Bartlett, I, ll.650-60.
11   *The Poems*, ed. Bartlett, I, 217, IV, ll.170-2.
12   'The Woods of Westermain', *The Poems*, ed. Bartlett, I, 217, IV, ll.167-8.
13   **Ode to the Spirit of Earth in Autumn**, l.184.
14   **The Lark Ascending**, l.112.
15   **The Thrush in February**, ll.142-4.
16   **Ode to the Spirit of Earth in Autumn**, ll.173-4.
17   **Ibid.**, ll.161-2.
18   'The Woods of Westermain', *The Poems*, ed. Bartlett, I, 213, IV, ll.19-20.
19   Cf. G. M. Trevelyan on this underlying mood; *Poetry and Philosophy*, pp.109-13.
20   *The Poems*, ed. Bartlett, I, 423, ll.14-16.

21   ll.77-80.
22   **Outer and Inner**, ll.30-1.
23   **Song in the Songless**, ll.1-4.
24   'The Empty Purse', *The Poems*, ed. Bartlett, I, 500, ll.591-2.

III STYLE
1   Letter to Augustus Jessopp, 20 September 1862; *Letters*, ed. Cline, I, 160.
2   **The Ordeal**, p. 250.
3   *Poetry and Philosophy*, p. 94.
4   *Autobiographies*, London, 1955, p. 167.
5   **Modern Love, XXV**, l.16.
6   Cf. the note below on **The Promise in Disturbance**.
7   l.14.
8   The version of 1878, ll.82 and 161.
9   Letter to Edmund Ollier, 8 or 9 July 1851; *Letters*, ed. Cline, I, 16.
10   ll.12-15.
11   ll.75-8.
12   Quoted by Crum, *Scientific Thought in Poetry*, p. 224.
13   Speaking of Meredith's prose, 26 February 1908; *Letters from Edward Thomas to Gordon Bottomley*, ed. R. George Thomas, London, 1968, p. 158.
14   Quoted by Lindsay, *George Meredith*, p. 348.
15   Lucas, 'Meredith as Poet', p. 17.
16   Bayley, 'The Puppet of a Dream', p. 1246.
17   'The State of Age', *The Poems*, ed. Bartlett, I, 291, ll.13-14.
18   Cf. Stevenson, *The Ordeal*, p. 346.
19   **Hard Weather**, ll.23-5.
20   **In the Woods**, ll.87-8.
21   ll.155-60.
22   Refrain: l.11, etc.
23   ll.1-2.
24   ll.12-15.
25   ll.89-90.
26   **Outer and Inner**, l.39.
27   Bernstein, *Precarious Enchantment*, p. 121.
28   'A Faith on Trial', *The Poems*, ed. Bartlett, I, 445, ll.554-6.
29   **Outer and Inner**, ll.19-20.
30   ll.8, 10, 33-4 and 80-2.

IV MODERN LOVE
1   **XVII**, l.12.
2   **XXX**, ll.13-16.
3   Cf. **XVIII**, l.9.

4   **XIII**, ll.1-3.
5   The 1878 version, l.44; despite the half-denial, ll.109-10.
6   **Ibid.**, ll.47-8.
7   **XLVII** ll.13-16.
8   'The Nuptials of Attila', *The Poems*, ed. Bartlett, I, 359, XXII, ll.13-15.
9   **L**, ll.1-2.
10 **L**, ll.11-12.
11 **XLIII**, ll.14-16.
12 **V**, l.4.
13 Cf. **X**, the centrally diagnostic sonnet.
14 **Ibid.**
15 Cf. **XXXI**.
16 **XLVIII**, l.10.
17 **XLIII**, ll.1-5.
18 **XLVII**, ll.3-4, 13-16. *And still I see* is the original version of 1862; after his second marriage he put it in the past tense.
19 **L**, ll.13-16.

V   INFLUENCES
1   'George Meredith', *Complete Poems of Hardy*, ed. Gibson, p.298, l.18.
2   Quoted by Stevenson, *Darwin Among the Poets*, p.203.
3   'A January Night', *Complete Poems of Hardy*, ed. Gibson, p.466, ll.7-8. The Meredithian quality of this and the following two poems is pointed out by Tom Paulin in *Thomas Hardy: The Poetry of Perception*, London, 1975, pp.156-7, and 163.
4   'To a Sea-Cliff', *Complete Poems of Hardy*, ed. Gibson, p.794, ll.19-24.
5   'Once at Swanage', *Complete Poems of Hardy*, ed. Gibson, p.784, ll.6-10.
6   **III**, l.15.
7   By Denis Donoghue, 'From the Country of the Blue', p.39.
8   Meredith's opinion of the characters in *The Holy Grail*; quoted by Lindsay, *George Meredith*, p.52.
9   Letter to Katharine Tynan; *The Letters of W. B. Yeats*, ed. Allan Wade, London, 1954, p.86.
10 Cf. A. Quiller-Couch, 'The Poetry of George Meredith', *Studies in Literature*, 1918, p.173.
11 Quoted by Donald Davie in *Thomas Hardy and British Poetry*, London, 1973, p.139.
12 *After Strange Gods*, London, 1934, p.48. Hopkins perhaps recognized the similarity of his 'The Sea and the Skylark', composed in 1877, and Meredith's 'The Lark Ascending' ; cf. W. H. Gardner, *Gerard Manley Hopkins (1844-1889): A Study of Poetic Idiosyncrasy in*

Relation to Poetic Tradition, 2 vols., London, 1949, II, 247n.

13 Letter to Frederick A. Maxse, 2 January 1870; *Letters*, ed. Cline, I, 412.

14 Cf. Ebbatson, *Lawrence and the Nature Tradition*, p.80.

15 'On Re-reading Meredith', *Collected Essays*, 4 vols., London, 1966-7, I, 234.

16 Cf. Donald Fanger, 'Joyce and Meredith: A Question of Influence and Tradition', *Modern Fiction Studies*. VI (1960), 125-30.

17 Quoted by Harriet Monroe, 'Meredith as Poet', *Poetry*, XXXII (1928), p.211.

18 [Vittoria's Concluding the Opera of 'Camilla'] , *The Poems*, ed. Bartlett, II, 852-3, ll.31-4.

19 Quoted by Siegfried Sassoon, *Meredith*, London, 1948, p.252.

THE POETRY

p.29 **Song: Spring** One of a group of 'Pastorals' in 1851.

p.29 **The Meeting** Originally published in *Once a Week*, 1 September 1862, illustrated by Millais. In the 'De Luxe' Edition, 1898, Meredith placed it among the 'Poems Written in Youth'. It was probably composed from 1849-51.

p.30 **The Promise in Disturbance** This prefatory sonnet was added to the reprinted *Modern Love*, 1892. In its place originally was the epigraph:

> This is not meat
> For little people or for fools.
> *Book of the Sages*

p.30 **Modern Love** The poem was composed between 1858 and 1862, that is, from the time Meredith's wife, Mary Ellen Nicolls, eloped with her lover, Henry Wallis, until several months after her death in October, 1861. Though the greater part appears to have been written in a few months after Mary's death, C. Day Lewis suggested the likelihood 'that its basic theme had been contemplated, many of its images formed, and perhaps a few detached sonnets written, before this' (ed., *Modern Love*, p.xvii).

The project was first mentioned in a letter on 19 November 1861 when the working title was probably 'A Love-Match'. About 17 January he sent F. Maxse 'a portion of proofs' of the poem he then called ' A Tragedy of Modern Love', and commented 'There are wanting to complete it, 13 more sonnets'. Phyllis Bartlett has pointed out that the poems sent to Maxse probably correspond to the 36 in a manuscript from the Altschul Meredith Collection of the Beinecke Library at Yale. There is evidence that Meredith rejected one of the original sonnets which does not appear in the Yale MS.

The original 37, therefore, together with the '13 more', would make up the sequence's full tally of 50; cf. 'A Manuscript of Meredith's "Modern Love" ', *Yale University Library Gazette*, XL (1966). Certainly the later poems and sonnet **X** (which was replaced by a completely different poem from the one in the Yale MS) were written after the letter of about 17 January. The poem under its final title was first published in May, 1862.

The sequence has an autobiographical basis in the gradual breakdown of Meredith's own marriage, though the real-life situation is considerably altered in the poem by a rigorous symmetry. Four characters are involved in the story—the husband and wife, and their respective lovers. For complex psychological and artistic reasons Meredith provides the husband with a consolatory affair with a blonde mistress, 'My Lady', which seems entirely unautobiographical. Indirectly, this invention may owe something to his infatuation with the young Janet Duff Gordon (the daughter of a baronet) after his wife's elopement, from 1858-60, when she married aged 18. But the sexual fulfilment of the liaison between the husband and his lady (cf. the note below on **XXXII**, l.4) is without counterpart in the author's own life. The relationship between the wife, referred to as 'Madam', and her friend, however, is left ambiguous (cf. **XXIV**), whereas it had been Mary's giving birth to an illegitimate child by Wallis that had forced the rupture between the Merediths. In a letter on 5 February 1892 Meredith wrote: 'As to the Lady [i.e. the wife] in 'Modern Love', her husband never accurately knew; therefore we ought not to inquire'. The wife's suicide, whether essential or not (cf. the note below on **XLVIII-L**), is a complete invention. Mary died of 'renal dropsy', a form of Bright's disease.

Meredith felt that in his treatment of the poem's personal theme he had won through to the representative status he implies for it in the final title. In a letter to an admirer on 20 September 1862, he describes it as essentially 'a dissection of the sentimental passion of these days'. The 'passion' analyzed in the poem is inseparable from the sceptical narrative tone and the experimental diversity of method, especially the emphasis on psychological reaction, which all contitute its *modernity*. Though formally and in its allusion to several Petrarchan conventions the poem's 50 16-line 'sonnets' (as Meredith himself referred to them, cf. **XXX**) derive ironically from the Renaissance sonnet sequence tradition of amatory courtship, several of its characteristic techniques are reminiscent rather of the short story; and several critics prefer to consider the sonnets as stanzas in a narrative, in the way of a Victorian verse-novel. The play between the discrete intensity of the individual sonnets and the simplifying continuities of the story-process lends the whole a problematic dimension. Recurrent images and verbal echoes between the sonnets bind them together, but they are given local definition which pays back into the reader's accumulating impressions. The narrative point of view is similarly puzzling. The sonnets are mostly spoken by the husband in the first person, but the opening 5 and the final 2 are spoken by a narrator who seems distinct from the husband. Occasionally, (cf. **VI** and **IX**), these viewpoints are mixed, so that the conflict between narration and dramatic monologue mimics the author's own dilemma of both telling and taking part in the story.

This problematic analysis, however, takes place within an overall sequence explained by Norman Friedman: through a time-span of just over a year, from spring (**XI**), to Christmas (**XXIII**), to summer (**XLV**), the story has 3 phases, ' (1) the development and amplification of the husband's ambivalence toward his wife' (**I-XXVI**), '(2) his attempt to find release in an affair with another woman' (**XXVII-XXXIX**), and '(3) his final and ill-fated reconciliation with his wife' (**XL-L**); cf. 'The Jangled Harp', p.10.

Jack Lindsay offers a paraphrase of the whole poem in *Life and Work*, pp.83-6.

p.30 **I** 15 *the sword between*: as Tristan and Isolde slept to preserve chastity. Ironically, the union between the husband and wife would be lawful; but it is unconsummated.

p.31 **II** 2-3 Cf. **XXXVI**, ll.13-15.

p.31 **III** 1 *the man*: the other man, whom the wife has begun to favour.

p.31 **IV** 1 *he*: the husband.

p.32 **VI** The first 2 and the last 2 lines are spoken by a narrator; the rest by the husband.

11 *barren*: metaphoric, but commencing a series of more poignant references to the couple's suggestive childlessness; cf. **XI**, ll.13-16, **XXI**, ll.13-14, and **XLVII**, ll.13-16. Mary had had a daughter by her first husband, and, after miscarriages or still births, the Merediths had had one legitimate son. It is just possible that the paternity of the son to whom Mary gave birth on 18 April 1858 may have been uncertain. The registration of his birth gave the father's name as 'George Meredith, author', though he was generally considered to have been Wallis's.

p.33 **VII** 4-8 and **VIII** 3 The serpent imagery recalls Bhanavar in the tale of Bhanavar and the Serpents, and the barber possibly the comic hero, Shibli Bagarag, both from Meredith's novel *The Shaving of Shagpat*, 1856.

p.33 **IX** The first 12 lines are spoken by a narrator; the last four by the husband.

13-14 He curses her, and at the same time acknowledges her happy beauty, like a sunbeam.

p.34 **X** Originally there was a completely different sonnet in this position which was later rejected, (see the introductory·note above on the Yale manuscript). The sonnet which now stands offers the most explicit diagnosis of the couple's incompatibility.

11-12 The husband claims that his wife resented his refusal to surrender to the sentimental myth of romantic love and his secret aspiration to achieve something in a wider context than their relationship, to make a contribution to society at large.

p.34 **XI** 13-16 Cf. **VI**, l.11.

p.35 **XII** 15 If I attempt to blank out any of my past experience.

p.35 **XIII** 15-16 *the . . . for ever* is a noun, the subject of *whirls*.

p.36 **XIV** From this sonnet on, the 'lady' refers to the woman with whom the husband is later to philander, and 'madam' to the wife.

5 *another veering fit*: his jealousy of his wife has been reversed: it is now her turn to experience it (9-10). 10 *her head*: his wife's.

p.36 **XV** 9-16 He shows her two letters: the first to himself, the second to the man she now favours.

p.36 **XVI** Probably an evocation of their time at the house of their convivial father-in-law, Thomas Love Peacock, at Lower Halliford on the Thames near Chertsey. They lived there a few months until summer 1853 when they moved across the village green to a cottage where they stayed until early 1856.

p.37 **XVII** 1-4 Reminiscent of the banquet scene in *Macbeth*, III. iv., where the host and 'honour'd hostess' (I. vi. 10) must 'make (their) faces vizards to (their) hearts,/Disguising what they are' (III. ii. 34-5). Lady Macbeth reproaches her husband: 'You do not give the cheer' (III. iv. 32), and the ghost of the murdered Banquo is seen only by the host. 12 *ephemerioe*: insects that live only for a day. Usually spelled 'ephemerae'. 14 Cf. Keats's 'Ode to a Nightingale', l.5: ''Tis not through envy of thy happy lot'. 16 *corpse-light*: 'ignis fatuus', the phosphorescence due to the spontaneous combustion of gases from decaying matter.

p.37 **XVII** and **XVIII** There was probably another sonnet between these two which was rejected and not replaced.

p.37 **XVIII** 6 *nut-brown stream*: ale. 11 Amphion was the legendary builder of Thebes. The music from his lute was so melodious that the stones danced into walls and houses of their own accord. As Bartlett notes, Meredith probably had in mind Tennyson's 'Amphion', where 'The gouty oak began to move,/ And flounder into hornpipes' (ll.23-4).

p.38 **XIX** 6-10 If I wish, though the nature of our relationship has changed fundamentally, to carry on mechanically making love (there is sexual overtone in 'time piece', 'can't stop' and 'swell'), the result will be impersonal lust.

p.38 **XX** 11 A love-token from a former flame.

p.39 **XXI** 6 An elliptic account of their friend's excited flow of conversation:—when the lady to whom he made his avowal said such and such ('this'): what ensued ('thus'): and how wonderful he thinks her. 13-14 Another ironic allusion to their childlessness; cf. note on **VI**, l.11.

p.39 **XXIII** 6 *the pit*: the unlit room; but also a site for primitive, almost bestial conflict. 9 His wife hostilely covers herself away from him.

p.40 **XXV** 9 *rosbif*: French for roast beef.

p.41 **XXVI** *A subtle serpent*: cf. Genesis 3:1.

pp.41-44 **XXVII-XXXIII** This group of sonnets refers to the lady.

p.41 **XXVII** 1-2 His doctor recommends an amatory diversion.

p.42 **XXIX** 2 *this head of gold*: the lady's. 3 *mould*: earth, the basic material of the human body; also, perhaps, the form imparted, rather than inherent. 4 *the consecration of the Past*: cf. Wordsworth, writing of his inability to preserve a precarious youthful vision, in 'Elegiac Stanzas Suggested by a Picture of Peele Castle', l.16: 'The consecration, and the Poet's dream'. 10 *Our human nakedness*: cf. Genesis 2:25, and 3:7.

p.42 **XXX** 9-11 Nature says: 'Those enjoying the fulfilments of love seem to be in closest contact with my essential principles; but in order to learn what those principles really are I will make them suffer a sense of loss and disillusionment'. 16 A sardonically modern critique of the Petrarchan love-sonnet conventions; cf. Shakespeare's sonnet CXXX, 'My mistress' eyes are nothing like the sun'.

p.43 **XXXI** 9-11 Carl H. Ketcham notes in the *Explicator*, XVII (1958), n.7: 'a reference to the celebrated "Count" Borowlaski . . . a Polish dwarf who, after successfully exhibiting himself for many years, died in Durham in 1837, aged ninety-eight. Walter Scott, in a letter to B. S. Morritt, July 24, 1814 . . . remarks that if Waverley had had married Flora, "she would have set him up upon the chimney-piece, as Count Borowlaski's wife used to do with him." The comparison, appropriate enough in itself, becomes markedly ironic if we assume that Meredith may have known the tiny Count's reputation for being witty, handsome, and successfully amorous—everything that the husband would wish to be in the eyes of "My Lady", reduced, in his abrupt mood of self-contempt, to ridiculous miniature'.

p.43 **XXXII** 4 *Bloom-covered*: an earlier MS reads 'Beneath me'. Meredith later seems to have wished to evade this explicitly sexual suggestion. 13-14 Cf. an earlier rejected reading: 'Woman is not her own cure'. This sense of frustration means that physical possession of a woman does not satisfy the complex craving which women provoke. 14 *the asp* is itself a small venomous serpent. 16 *Bacchantes*:

orgiastic female votaries of Bacchus, god of wine.

p.43 **XXXIII** 1-3 The painting referred to is by Raphael, 'St Michael and the Devil'. 5-6 In the battle of Pharsalia, 48BC, Pompey's huge host was decisively beaten by Caesar's modest forces. As Bartlett notes: 'It would seem (Meredith) meant the Romans of Pompey's army rather than "Pharsalians" . . . The inexperienced young aristocrats in Pompey's army were given to luxury, self-indulgence, and fear of disfigurement. They were slow to join battle and quick to retreat'. 8 *still*: constantly. 1 1 *these worms*: men. 12 *he*: 'the Fiend'.

p.44 **XXXIV** 7-8 *Niagara* Falls and the active volcano, *Vesuvius*, are made metaphors for the coming explosive rupture.

p.44 **XXXV** 10-12 A premonition of her suicide.

p.45 **XXXVI** 13-15 Cf. **II**, ll.2-3.

p.45 **XXXVII** Probably another evocation of Lower Halliford; cf. the note on **XVI**. 4 *the chariot*: the sun; Apollo, god of the sun, was supposed to ride in a seven-horse chariot.

p.46 **XXXVIII** 1ff. Addressed to the lady. 5 *Gogmagos*: giants. In British legend, Gog and Magog are the last of a hoard of monstrous giants, the offspring of demons; and in *Revelation* they symbolize all future enemies of the Kingdom of God. Here the compound stands for the greatest sensualists, who are imposing but unadmirable. 12 *that woman*: his wife.

p.46 **XXXIX** 1-2 She accedes to the proposition in the previous sonnet—accepts his fully mature love. 4 A reminiscence of the wooing of his wife; cf. **XL**, l.11.

p.46 **XL** 6 *amain*: with full force. 11 *of maidenhood*: Mary was a young widow, Meredith's elder by nearly 7 years, when they married.

p.47 **XLI** 11-12 They decide to make love according to the letter of their marriage-vows, and to renounce their new, more vibrant loves.

p.47 **XLII** 8 *Pallas*: Minerva, the warrior-goddess of wisdom. 13 *Hebe*: the goddess of youth. She was supposed to have the power of restoring youth and vigour. *Thoughts black as death*: cf. the Player as Lucianus in *Hamlet*. He is about to poison Gonzago before getting the love of his victim's wife: 'Thoughts black, hands apt, drugs fit, and time agreeing' (III. ii. 266).

p.48 **XLIV** 7 *Poor soul*: his wife. 7-8 If when our relationship first began to break up I had been only hurt, rather than goaded into alienation . . . . 11-12 She entered into a bargain which entailed the return of love, and considers pity no fair substitute.

p.49 **XLVI** 9 *not alone*: as a result of the explanation with her husband, she has arranged to meet the other man. 12 His anxiety that her rendezvous was amatory and that she would accordingly react guiltily or with hostility on his approach proved unfounded and died away.

p.49 **XLVII** 1 Cf. Keats's 'To Autumn', l.33: 'And gathering swallows twitter in the skies'. 9-12 Possibly a subconscious suggestion of indelible horror in the reminiscence of Lady Macbeth's: 'No, this hand will rather/The multitudinous seas incarnadine,/Making the green one red' (*Macbeth*, II. ii. 60-2). 13-16 Cf. note on **VI**, l.11. 15 *Where I have seen*: 'And still I see' in 1862.

p.50 **XLVIII** 9-12 When they discussed the lady he had given up, his wife, from confused and self-wounding impulses of unsophisticated instinct, ran away in order to break down the restraints their relationship imposed on his supposed desire for the other woman. 15 *sentience*: sensitive understanding.

pp.50-51 **XLVIII** 13-16, **XLIX**, and **L** Bartlett notes Wilfred Blunt's entry for 7 November 1905, where he records Wilfred Meynell's expounding of the poem, 'as Meredith had expounded it to Mrs Meynell. According to this the last two stanzas mean that the wife, 'madam', commits suicide so as to leave the poet free to marry 'My Lady.' [Sydney] Cockerell thinks that to have been an afterthought, and that the wife eloped with her lover. Meredith, Meynell says, seems to have persuaded himself that his wife, in real life, left him for some such altruistic motive, but this must have been self-delusion, as she certainly lived with her lover till her death' (*My Diaries*, 2 vols., London, 1919-20, II, 125). Mary and Wallis, in fact, separated after their return to England.

p.50 **XLIX** 4 A source of joy, but also insecurity as to whether it was genuine and lasting. 7-8 She is terrified that she will have to confront fully the realization she already faintly acknowledges: that the renewed relationship is an illusion, for both. 12 *awful*: filled with awe or solemn respect. *Lethe*: one of the rivers of Hades which the souls of the dead are obliged to taste, so that they may forget everything said and done when alive. She has taken poison.

p.51 **L** 3-4 Cf. 'I Chafe at Darkness', ll.13-15. *flitting*: fluttering, on short, swift flights. 11-16 Bayley suggests ('The Puppet of a Dream', p.1248) this ending echoes Byron's 'Lines on Hearing that Lady Byron was Ill', ll.9-12:

> It is not in the storm nor in the strife
> We feel benumbed, and wish to be no more,
> But in the after-silence on the shore,
> When all is lost, except a little life.

p.51 **The Old Chartist** Originally published in *Once a Week*, 8 February 1862, illustrated by Frederick Sandys. Composed before 12 June 1861.

The Chartist movement was founded by a group of skilled workmen, and in 1838 drew up the People's Charter—a 6-point programme of political reforms. Its demands were universal manhood suffrage, equal electoral districts, vote by ballot, annually elected parliaments, payment of MPs, and the abolition of property qualifications for membership of parliament. Two opposed strategies were advocated by the 'physical force school' and the 'moral force' men, who wished the petition to go through by peaceful means. Parliament rejected their claims; but, in 1842, the petition was re-presented, and the movement involved itself in the strikes which resulted from the trade depression. The climax of the movement came in 1848, the year of bad harvests in Britain and revolutions abroad, with a planned march of half a million on London. In the event, a much smaller body of marchers was resisted by the military, and rigorous precautions taken by the authorities. Thereafter, though it survived in the provinces over the following decade, the movement petered out, largely due to improving economic conditions, and its activists joined allied causes such as trade unionism, cooperation, Irish nationalism, and middle-class radical agitation for a wider franchise. Only 19 English and Welsh Chartists were actually transported.

Meredith's earlier poem, 'Brotherhood', published in *The Monthly Observer*, March 1849, had more topically demonstrated his allegiance to the broad issues of liberty and egalitarianism which the movement had stood for. The subject of this poem appreciates the changed conditions of relative prosperity in mid-Victorian Britain, with his daughter marrying into the lower middle-classes; but he still insists on the relevance of his basic old convictions.

1 *dam*: mother. 22 *his Grace's*: a local duke's. 56 *lawny*: lawn is the fabric used for the sleeves of an Anglican bishop's official dress. 60 *doubled* and 62 *seconding*: he is reflected in the river as in a looking-glass. 77 *supple*: ingratiating, obsequious. 90 *To screw me for my work*: to brace him for the trial. 93-4 His political argumentation is lubricated by tea-drinking (as opposed to alcohol). 102 and 115-16 Compare Meredith's reductive symbol of democracy with the 'cosmopolitan sympathies' of Isaac Rosenberg's 'sardonic' and 'droll rat' in 'Break of Day in the Trenches', ll.7-8.

p.55 **I Chafe at Darkness** 13-15 Cf. *Modern Love*, L, ll.3-4. 15-18 Cf. *Modern Love*, **XXIX**, ll.5-14.

p.55 **Ode to the Spirit of Earth in Autumn** Several passages are based on parts of an early long poem, 'Wandering Willie', which Meredith began in 1848/9, and abandoned in a fragmentary form in 1854. Canto 2 of the original long poem was influenced strongly by the Wanderer's rhapsodies in Wordsworth's *The Excursion* and by the poetry of the Spasmodic poets. The ode is also reminiscent in conception and imagery of 'South-West Wind in the Woodland', published 1851, and of 'The South-Wester', published 1888.

1-18 An extended description of 'Autumn's sunset skies' (2). 33-5 The spirits, mounted on sea-horses, ride past the ships (hulls) lying side by side, as at a military inspection (review), with their prows (beaks) bobbing in the sea. 49 *Dryad*: as of wood-nymphs. 112 *the Anakim*: the aboriginal giants of southern Palestine, according to the Old Testament. 113 *acclaiming to*: shouting applause to. 150 *for*: because of. 158 *Bacchante*: cf. the note on *Modern Love*, **XXXII**, l.16. 174-5 In 1862 there were 45 more lines here, later deleted by Meredith.

p.61 **A Ballad of Past Meridian** Originally published in the *Fortnightly*, 1 June 1876. *Meridian* is mid-day, noon; also the climacteric of his own life.

p.62 **The Lark Ascending** Originally published in the *Fortnightly*, 1 May 1881. It is reminiscent, in treatment, of Shelley's 'To a Skylark'. But Meredith seems to expatiate on the theme of Wordsworth's 'To a Skylark', 'Type of the wise who soar, but never roam;/True to the kindred points of Heaven and Home' (ll.11-12), to reply to Shelley's scepticism about the human relevance of the bird's oblivious joy.

1 *to round*: to move in a circular course. 44 *argentine*: silvery material. 99-122 Reminiscent of Wordsworth's 'Character of the Happy Warrior' and 'Toussaint L'Ouverture', ll.9-14, in its mingling of natural process and human resolution. 109-112 These lines seem to answer Shelley's appeal in 'To a Skylark', ll.101-5:

> Teach me half the gladness
> > That thy brain must know,
> Such harmonious madness
> > From my lips would flow,
> The world would listen then, as I am listening now.

110 *pass*: exceed. 119 The spiralling flight images the integration of a broadening horizontal human scope and a vertical aspiration towards the concave of the sky (dome).

p.65 **Love in the Valley** This, the second of the two versions of the poem, first appeared in *Macmillan's*, October 1878. The original version is printed in an appendix above (p.96).

The title probably derives from Tennyson's idyll in *The Princess*, 1847, 'Come down, O maid, from yonder mountain height', ll.183-5:

> And come, for Love is of the valley, come
> For Love is of the valley, come thou down
> And find him.

The metre, which Meredith himself describes in a note as 'Trochaic, variable in short syllables according to stress of the accent', is thought to have been adapted from George Darley's 'Serenade of a Loyal Martyr', which first appeared in the *Athenaeum*, 23 January 1836.

Stevenson refutes the idea that it was inspired by Meredith's wooing of his first wife, Mary Ellen Nicolls: 'All the evidence points to memories of a boyish episode as the source of the ecstatic note . . . ' (*The Ordeal*, p.35).

1-8 The situation of the poet's watching the sleeping girl is also that of Darley's 'Serenade'. 36 *evejar*: or nightjar. 61 *shows the South-West*: if the South-West . . . . 75 *Rounding*: cf. the note on **The Lark Ascending**, l.1. 77 The bird is lost in the pink dawn sky which is making the morning star invisible; cf. the note on **Hymn to Colour**, l.13. 95 *rolling dumb for thunder*: perhaps the distant rumbling (like a drum-roll) is followed by a pause before the thunder-clap. 105-12: Cf. Keats's 'The Eve of St. Agnes', ll.262-79, for a similar transference of the sleeping girl's sensuousness to associated inanimate objects—here sweet-smelling flowers; in Keats, sweetmeats. 117 *yaffle*: green woodpecker. 118 Geoffrey Tillotson notes that the line is 'derived from Ruskin's chapter, 'The Truth of Chiaroscuro', in *Modern Painters*, II. II. iii, 'especially such a remark as "For no out-line of objects whatsoever is so sharp as the edge of a close shadow"'' (*Criticism and the Nineteenth Century*, London, 1951, p.33n). 121-4 Cf. Donne's Elegy XIX, 'Going to Bed', ll.13-14: 'Your gown going off such beauteous state reveals/As when from flowry meads the sun's shadow steals'. 148 *the blue*: the sky. 162 *Clipped*: embraced; also pared down at the edge, like a coin of precious metal. 165-6 The tree gazes on the shadows cast (printed) on the ground by the moonlight shining through the branches. 187-8 The image of the sheaves leads into the notion of the girl's dress and hair being un-bound like a sheaf. 197 *the wild white cherry*: cf. 'A Faith on Trial', ll.218-30.

p.71 **The Orchard and the Heath** Originally published in *Macmillan's*, 17 February 1868, where it formed Part 1 of a two-part poem. The sceond part was omitted in 1883.

p.72 **Lucifer in Starlight** Lucifer is both the Morning Star and another name for Satan; cf. Isaiah 14:12ff. The sonnet is Miltonic in form.

7 *Afric's sands*: 'Africa' in 1883. *careened*: leaned over on one side, like a boat; cf. Satan's flight in *Paradise Lost*, II, ll.1041-44. 9 *his scars*: cf. Satan's face, in *Paradise Lost*, which 'Deep scars of thunder had intrenched' (II, l.601). 14 Cf. Eliot's 'Cousin Nancy', where this line is quoted ironically to evoke the authority of Arnold and Emerson as touchstones of New England conventions.

p.73 **A Later Alexandrian** The subject of this sonnet is probably Dante Gabriel Rossetti who died in 1882, the year before its publication. Meredith had sometimes stayed in rooms he rented in Rossetti's bohemian household in Chelsea for about half a year in 1862-3. His first wife's lover, Henry Wallis, painted also in the vividly colour-ful Pre-Raphaelite manner.

Alexandrian: belonging to the final phase and decline of Greek civilization; characterized by a sense of recondite artificiality. 7-8 Rossetti's beautiful tubercular wife committed suicide the year before he moved to Chelsea.

p.73 **King Harald's Trance** Originally entitled, in a fair copy, 'The Trance of Harald Hammerskull'. Bartlett notes that this hero is the subject of Johann Ludwig Uhland's poem, *Harald*, 1853, where he 'is left sitting on a stone in a permanent sleep; occasionally he brandished his sword'.

I-V Trevelyan summarizes: 'King Harald, after excessive exertions in battle and feasting, falls into a trance'. 1 *amain*: with all his might; violently. 19 *awink*: adverb, 'winking'. VI-XII Trevelyan summarizes: 'Awakening from it, but still unable to move or speak, he lies silent and hears treason talked at the side of his couch by his wife and a warrior'. 31-2 This 'god of war' did not have enough strength to bleat like a lamb. 44 *him*: himself. XIII-XVI Trevelyan summarizes: 'With a final effort he bursts the bands of his trance enough to cut down his wife dead'. 58 *that proof of life*: his breath shown on the cold blade. 59 *netters*: fishermen with nets. 62 *the blow clove two*: his wife was pregnant; cf. 35-6. XVII-XVIII Trevelyan summarizes: 'Then his life-force snaps and he falls dead before he can slay "the third" (63), her lover'.

p.76 **Hard Weather** 3 *shaws*: strips of woods forming the boundaries of fields. 9 *shrews*: makes the sound of the mouse-like mammal, the shrew; also, curses, scolds. 13 *accost*: greeting. 16 *Tritonly*: in the manner of a Triton, a sea-deity. 29 *the Furies*: the 3 avenging goddesses. 30 *The Fates*: the 3 goddesses supposed to determine the course of human life. 33 The wind, which bore the seed from which grew the vegetation it now devastates. 36-9 Cf. Genesis 32: 24-30. 53-4 The character of human fortitude is retained in its evolution from brawn to brain. 65 *dagger-day*: time of conflict. 68 *drill*: rigorous military training; with overtones of whirling round, and making the seed-furrow. 89 *rive*: tear apart.

p.79 **The Thrush in February** Originally published in *Macmillan's*, August 1885. It was written, as was 'A Faith on Trial' later the same year, while Meredith's second wife was dying from throat cancer.

4 *bines*: twining stems 5 Before the song of the returning migratory birds starts. 16 *the deluge-ebb*: the ebb perhaps of the spring-flood; but also perhaps of Noah's flood. 23 *clear in pale*: clear but colourless (washed out). 24 *beck*: small stream. 27-8 A piece of lighter, sun-lit, sky will show through the clouds, which are less bright, as if it is being unshelled, like a pearl, or having a veil lifted from its face. 40 The sky seems actively to be assuming darkness, though it takes a long time before it becomes completely dark. 45 *me*: to me. 56 *pricked with*: tormented by. 69 *that*:

i.e. 'the forward view'. 85 *mark*: specific aim. 95/137 *the sighting brain*: the mind growing more perceptive. 101 *ventral*: of the belly. 109-10 Though at present the men who are wise in watching Earth pass seemingly ineffectually, such men are controlling and bringing the future into being. 111-12 Earth continues producing the same old vegetational cycle; but those who are to grow and aspire with her essential life are those activated by a rational sense of their individuality. 115-16 Earth punishes those who object loudly to the obscurity of human destiny for not accepting the active responsibility of shaping it. She leaves them to suffer from the specifically human rational realization of their predicament. 119 *past*: beyond. 125 *to speed*: to cause to prosper. 140-1 Earth, whom materialists consider inanimate matter, idealists as phantom spirit, transcends this dualism, and is not just an emblem of the life-force which she herself inherently is.

p.84 **Outer and Inner** 11-12 The bells on the foxgloves become smaller the nearer the tips, and each day he passes bells have fallen, beginning with the heavier, lower ones. 18 Hushed, I observe the minutest (details). 35-6 *have we . . . have we*: if we have . . . .

p.85 **Dirge in Woods** Originally published in the *Fortnightly*, 1 August 1870, as stanza IX of 'In the Woods'; cf. the note below on that poem. It was written on the death of Meredith's second father-in-law, and is a close imitation of Goethe's 'Uber allen Gipfeln' ('Wandrers Nachtlied II').

7 *its dead*: the non-fertilized seed.

p.85 **Change in Recurrence** An elegy on his second wife.

12 The mischievous blackbird became as plump as a chough. 17-18 The scene is now like the background of a portrait from which his wife's face is missing. 19 She no longer throws open the window to call his name.

p.86 **Hymn to Colour** Basil de Sélincourt and Trevelyan offer a stanza by stanza explication; and M. R. Ridley one of the first 7 stanzas. Trevelyan notes: 'A dualism runs through the thought of this poem. Light, Darkness, and Colour answer respectively to Life, Death, and Love. Colour is to Light and Darkness as Love is to Life and Death'. The setting is probably the Swiss Alps; and the poem evokes the transition from early dawn to sunrise.

13 *the dark-winged planet*: the planet Venus, the morning star, sometimes referred to as 'Lucifer', synonymous with the fallen angel; cf. 'Lucifer in Starlight', l.9. 15-16 The star's radiance is affected by the dawning light, so that it seems smaller and farther away rather than dimmer, remaining whiter than the lightening sky. Meredith commented on this line: 'If you observe the Planet Venus at the hour when the dawn does no more than give an intimation, she is

full of silver, and darkness surrounds her. So she seems to me to fly on dark wings . . . "Black Star" is common in classic poets. It is true I push the epithet farther. But so I saw it' (Letter to J. C. Smith, 14 May 1907; *Letters*, ed. Cline, III, 1595). **17-18** The colouring of dawn suffuses Life and Death, so that they merge, as alternate threads, into one (cloud-like) tenuously woven substance, lightly rising and falling. **19-20** The sun has not yet appeared; but the colouring of dawn is thrown over the snowy shoulders of the peaks like a mantle. **25-30** Can a man understand the mystery of life through the sensation of his own organic vitality? Or learn the secret of death by examining a corpse? Only by the constant activity of straining to realize his increasing potentialities of mind and body can a man participate in the universal process. Cf. **The Thrush in February**, ll.105-14. **31-6** This stanza is filled with images of promised integration. The central image is that of the marriage between the beauty of the physical world revealed in colour and the imaginative potential of man's mind. As this occurs, there is both an emotional release and a sense of gently achieved poise (*knotting arms*), intimating a universal order (*boundless*). **43-4** *his*: i.e. Colour's. **45** *He*: Colour. **53-4** The 'bloom of dawn' soon passes, but the memory of it pervades all that follows after. **55** You are no sooner seen than you pass away. **61** *the emissary eglantine*: the yellowish haze of the sweet-briers is the first sight of day. **63** *thy star*: the morning star; cf. note on 13 above. **69-70** Who think the potential of 'rapt desire' is terminated by the intensity of its sudden access. **74** *spell*: make out with difficulty. **79** *than any lost*: i.e. the lost paradise of Eden. **81** Alluding to the theory of Man's ape-like origin.

p.89 **The Lesson of Grief** **2** *ages*: a verb: which makes the recollection of happy past times seem old and worn.

p.89 **Night of Frost in May** Meredith extracted this separate poem from a two-part original entitled 'The Poet's Night', the rest of which he left unpublished. Bartlett dates its composition about 1890. There is a pervasive reminiscence of Coleridge's 'Frost at Midnight', in setting, and in the poise of natural and human worlds.

3 *night*: a pun on 'knight'. **13** Describing the formation of an icicle: the sense of vital movement (the small fish, or minnow) within the fluid vehicle (the small rill), whose fluency is impeded (limping) by the icicle's freezing. **15-36** A description of the song of nightingales. **17** *elude*: slip away from perception. **21** The poet holds his breath and stands still to listen attentively. **41-2** A composite ecstasy of song unites the individually competitive voices of multitudinous (legion) birds. **49-50** The sharp sensation of breathing in cold air prevented me from receding into internal fantasy when the world round me provided an imaginative experience open to real

116

sensory perception. 50 *visionary gleam*: cf. Wordsworth's 'Ode: Intimations of Immortality', l.5: 'Whither is fled the visionary gleam?' 55-6 The nightingales' song is a composite of joy and woe; and though neither of these feelings arises from human experience, nevertheless they seem to objectify them. 56 *plained*: lamented. 58 Harmonized, as in a chord, disparate elements. 61 The song has taken his realist experience to a point that enables spiritual transcendence. 64 *As had a star*: As if a star had .... 64-6 *the spheres*: the outward limits of space where the celestial bodies appear to have their place. Pythagoras theorized that the planets there make sounds according to their different rates of motion, and that these sounds harmonize. The golden age was expected to return when these sounds became audible on earth. Meredith's idea here is that a star has attracted the earth to a position half-way between its usual one and that of the spheres, where the stars can be seen intensely bright, and the spheres are close enough for their fabled music to be heard. 73 *dead-ebb shores*: the lowest state of the tide, when it has receded its farthest. 75 A rejected version gives: 'But would I now revive it . . . '; cf. Coleridge's 'Kubla Khan', ll.42-7: 'Could I revive within me/Her symphony and song . . . '. In the unpublished second part of the original poem, among the roll-call of poets he associates with the scene, is Coleridge, 'who gave to ear/"A damsel with a dulcimer" ', from the same poem. 76 *issue notes*: the nightingales' song which emanated from the scene. 77 *serious*: manifesting some earnest purpose, and open to considered analysis; with a sense of importance. 81-2 The frozen ice-drop on the top leaf of the bending fern (the bracken-crook).

p.92 **In the Woods** This poem is the remains of a much longer one entitled 'In the Woods. Foresight and Patience', probably composed 1868-70. Part was published under the original title in the *Fortnightly*, 1 August 1870, and was subsequently dismembered to form separate, much altered, shorter poems: 'Whimper of Sympathy', 'Woodland Peace' and **Dirge in Woods**. The remaining 6 sections were published by Trevelyan in the form given here. The rest of the original poem, the dialogue 'Foresight and Patience', was published as a complete, separate poem in *A Reading of Life*, 1901.

23 *fold*: an enclosure for sheep; and also a group of adherents to a common creed. 29 *self-hunted in it*: isolated, in the darkness, into a sense of individual identity. 53-60 Cf. **Dirge in Woods**, ll.7-15.

p.96 **Aimée** First published by Bartlett.

5 *shot*: bullet. *sounded*: got to the bottom of.

p.96 **Love in the Valley**, 1851 This, the first of the two versions, was published in 1851. The text printed is the slightly corrected one of the 'De Luxe' edition, 1898. Cf. the note above on the second version.

10 *athwart*: across.   65 *the grey star*: the morning star; cf. the note on **Hymn to Colour**, l.13.   78 *Waits*: Awaits.   82 *crescent brows*: newly emerging natural appearances.   84 May we be married by the end of the month, when the new moon will have become full.

SELECTED BIBLIOGRAPHY

George Meredith: A Bibliography, Michael Collie, Folkestone, 1974.

The Ordeal of George Meredith, Lionel Stevenson, London, 1954. (Biography).

The Letters of George Meredith, ed. C. L. Cline, 3 vols., Oxford, 1970.

Bayley, John: 'The Puppet of a Dream', the *Times Literary Supplement*, 27 October 1978, pp.1246-8. (Review article)

Beach, Joseph Warren: 'Meredith' in *The Concept of Nature in Nineteenth-Century English Poetry*, New York, 1956.

Bernstein, Carol L.: *Precarious Enchantment: A Reading of Meredith's Poetry*, Washington, 1979.

Cosslett, Tess: 'Meredith' in *The 'Scientific Movement' in Victorian Literature*, Brighton, Sussex, 1982.

Crum, Ralph B.: 'The Poet's Dilemma—Reason or Mysticism' in *Scientific Thought in Poetry*, New York, 1931.

Crunden, Patricia: 'The Woods of Westermain', *Victorian Poetry*, V (1967), pp.265-82.

Donoghue, Denis: 'From the Country of the Blue', the *New York Review of Books*, 22 February 1979, pp.37-9. (Review article).

Ebbatson, Roger: 'George Meredith' in *Lawrence and the Nature Tradition: A Theme in English Fiction 1859-1914*, Sussex and New Jersey, 1980.

Friedman, Norman: 'The Jangled Harp: Symbolic Structure in *Modern Love*', *Modern Language Quarterly*, XVIII (1957), pp.9-26.

Kelvin, Norman: *A Troubled Eden: Nature and Society in the Works of G. Meredith*, Edinburgh, 1961.

Leavy, Barbara Fass: 'The Romanticism of Meredith's "Love in the Valley" ', *Studies in Romanticism*, XVIII (1979), pp.99-113.

Lindsay, Jack: *George Meredith, His Life and Work*, London, 1956.

Lucas, John: 'Meredith as Poet' in *Meredith Now: Some Critical Essays*. ed. Ian Fletcher, London, 1971.

Mermin, Dorothy M.: 'Poetry as Fiction: Meredith's *Modern Love*', English Literary History, XLIII (1976) pp.100-19.

Perkus, Gerald H.: 'Meredith's Unhappy Love Life: Worthy of the Muse', *Cithara*, IX (1970), pp.32-46.

Reader, Willie D.: 'Stanza Form in *Modern Love*', *Victorian Newsletter*, XXXVIII (1970), pp.26-7.

Ridley, M. R.: 'Meredith's Poetry' in *Second Thoughts: More Studies in Literature*, London, 1965.

Simpson, Arthur L., Jr.: 'Meredith's Pessimistic Humanism: A New Reading of *Modern Love*',*Modern Philology*, LXVII (1970),pp.314-56.

Stevenson, L.: 'George Meredith' in *Darwin Among the Poets*, Chicago, 1932.

Stone, James: 'Meredith and Goethe', *University of Toronto Quarterly*, XXI (1952), pp.157-66.

Trevelyan, G. M.: *The Poetry and Philosophy of George Meredith*, London, 1906.

Williams, Ioan: ed. *Meredith: the Critical Heritage*, London, 1971.

Wilson, Phillip E.: 'Affective Coherence, A Principle of Abated Action, and Meredith's *Modern Love*', *Modern Philology*, LXXII (1974), pp.151-71.

"The Fyfield Books series provides an admirable service in publishing good inexpensive selections from the works of interesting but neglected poets"
— *British Book News*

WALTER SAVAGE LANDOR (1775-1864)
Selected Poems and Prose
edited by Keith Hanley

ANDREW MARVELL (1621-78)
Selected Poems
edited by Bill Hutchings

GEORGE MEREDITH (1828-1909)
Selected Poems
edited by Keith Hanley

CHARLES OF ORLEANS (1394-1465)
Selected Poems
edited by Sally Purcell

SIR WALTER RALEGH (?1554-1618)
Selected Writings
edited by Gerald Hammond

JOHN WILMOT, EARL OF ROCHESTER
(1648-80)
The Debt to Pleasure
edited by John Adlard

CHRISTINA ROSSETTI (1830-94)
Selected Poems
edited by C.H. Sisson

SIR PHILIP SIDNEY (1554-86)
Selected Poetry and Prose
edited by Richard Dutton

JOHN SKELTON (1460-1529)
Selected Poems
edited by Gerald Hammond

CHRISTOPHER SMART (1722-71)
Selected Poems
edited by Marcus Walsh

DONALD STANFORD (editor)
Three Poets of the Rhymers' Club:
Lionel Johnson, Ernest Dowson,
John Davidson

HENRY HOWARD, EARL OF SURREY
(1517-47)
Selected Poems
edited by Dennis Keene

JONATHAN SWIFT (1667-1745)
Selected Poems
edited by C.H. Sisson

ALGERNON CHARLES SWINBURNE
(1837-1909)
Selected Poems
edited by L.M. Findlay

ARTHUR SYMONS (1865-1945)
Selected Writings
edited by R.V. Holdsworth

THOMAS TRAHERNE (?1637-74)
Selected Writings
edited by Dick Davis

HENRY VAUGHAN (1622-95)
Selected Poems
edited by Robert B. Shaw

ANNE FINCH, COUNTESS OF WINCHILSEA
(1661-1720)
Selected Poems
edited by Denys Thompson

EDWARD YOUNG (1683-1765)
Selected Poems
edited by Brian Hepworth

"Carcanet are doing an excellent job in this series: the editions are labours of love, not just commercial enterprises. I hope they are familiar to all readers and teachers of literature." – *Times Literary Supplement*